STORM BEAT

STORM BEAT

A Journalist Reports from the Oregon Coast

Lori Tobias

Oregon State University Press   Corvallis

Library of Congress Cataloging-in-Publication Data

Names: Tobias, Lori, author.
Title: Storm beat : a journalist reports from the Oregon coast / Lori
    Tobias.
Other titles: Oregonian (Portland, Or. : 1937)
Description: Corvallis : Oregon State University Press, 2020.
Identifiers: LCCN 2020027023 (print) | LCCN 2020027024 (ebook) | ISBN
    9780870710117 (trade paperback) | ISBN 9780870710148 (ebook)
Subjects: LCSH: Tobias, Lori. | Journalists—United States—Biography. |
    Pacific Coast (Or.)
Classification: LCC PN4874.T57 A3 2020 (print) | LCC PN4874.T57 (ebook) |
    DDC 070.4/49975—dc23
LC record available at https://lccn.loc.gov/2020027023
LC ebook record available at https://lccn.loc.gov/2020027024

∞ This paper meets the requirements of ANSI/NISO Z39.48-1992
(Permanence of Paper).

First published in 2020 by Oregon State University Press
Printed in the United States of America

Oregon State University
OSU Press

Oregon State University Press
121 The Valley Library
Corvallis OR 97331-4501
541-737-3166 • fax 541-737-3170
www.osupress.oregonstate.edu

For Chan, who makes it all possible.

CONTENTS

AUTHOR'S NOTE

The stories here are based on my collection of reporter's notes and the journals I kept almost daily during the years I was on staff at the *Oregonian* and beyond. The facts—prices, community descriptions, statistics, etc.—reflect the period in which the stories took place, and may well have changed over time.

PROLOGUE

The murder victim's sister-in-law was working the register at Fred Meyer. Seeing me, she smiled and nodded hello in that courteous grocery-store-clerk way. Barb knew me as Chan's wife, spouse of the man who worked with her husband. I took a breath and began. "Barb, my name's Lori Tobias." She gave me a blank look. "I write for the *Oregonian*."

Now, Barb looked up from beneath her dark brown bangs. Our eyes met, and I saw the instant flutter of panic. "I'm writing about Jenny and Kara." Her eyes filled, a tear spilled over and ran down her cheek, then another. She wiped at her face and looked away, and then my eyes filled, too.

Some days I hated my job.

I'd never meant to pursue journalism on the Oregon coast. Rather, I'd planned to write: A novel. Essays. Perhaps a feature now and again. The writing I loved. But no, not news.

I had come to the coast by way of Pennsylvania, Alaska, Connecticut, Seattle, southern Oregon, and finally, Colorado, where I had a Sunday column and wrote features for the *Rocky Mountain News*. My husband Chan was a power lineman, and so we followed the big construction line jobs. Tramping, they call it. People felt bad for me moving all the time. I thought I was lucky. Every new town was a fresh adventure, even the grocery store. We explored everything we could while we had the chance, because we always knew before long we'd be gone. We were, by Paul Bowles's definition, not tourists, but travelers: "Whereas the tourist generally hurries back home at the end of a few weeks or months, the traveler belonging no more to one place than to the next, moves slowly over periods of years, from one part of the earth to another."

I found that quote in his book *The Sheltering Sky*, and instantly recognized myself. I belonged nowhere. I belonged everywhere. I wasn't sure I would ever stay in one place, but if we ever did settle down we always said it would be on the Oregon coast. That was our mantra.

In 2000, just as the *Rocky Mountain News* entered into a Joint Operating Agreement (JOA) with the *Denver Post* that cast the *Rocky* as the "loser," just as I hit a milestone year, forty, just as the one-year anniversary of the Columbine High School massacre came and went, I saw a help-wanted ad for a lineman at a central coast utility and fired off my husband's resume. That was on a Monday. One week later, he interviewed with the Central Lincoln People's Utility District (PUD) by phone. We flew to Portland Thursday and drove to the coast, where I wrote my Sunday column for the *Rocky* from a third-story hotel room overlooking the beach. It was foggy and gray, and I thought it was beautiful and romantic and somehow a bit poignant. That night we slept with the hotel room deck door open—electric Cadet heater blazing—so we could better hear the surf. I knew there was a good chance we would move here, and the idea both thrilled and saddened me. In Denver, I was invited to restaurant openings, box seats at pro sports games, elite private parties, and social events. I was not the small-town Pennsylvania daughter of a truck driver and waitress, neither of whom had graduated from high school; I was Lori Tobias with the *Rocky Mountain News*, first- and second-place winner that year for features and magazine writing from the Colorado Society of Journalists. Who would I be on the Oregon coast?

I knew that answer all too well. I would be another struggling writer with the dream of publishing my novel, a dream with a slim, slim chance of coming true. On staff at a newspaper or magazine, my work would be published and read. On my own, there were no such guarantees.

They offered Chan the job that afternoon.

The Oregon coast. It was supposed to be our version of paradise. We bought a house with views of the ocean set against a backdrop of towering evergreens and a profusion of flowers that bloomed wild nearly year round: calla lilies, hydrangeas, rhododendrons, azaleas. A place where traffic jams were two rounds at the same red light and violent crime the exception.

And I was miserable. I loved the beauty of the Oregon coast, but I couldn't quite get my head around the idea that this was the end of the road. And I missed the Denver newsroom, missed the parties, the openings, the sun and the snow, even the pro sports games. And I missed my friends. I moved from a city where the phone book filled two volumes, each as thick as a brick, to one where you could fit the entire directory in a space as slender as a reporter's pad. Voice mail was not an option, and a phone call twenty miles away was long distance. For shopping, there was Fred Meyer, Walmart, and for a time, a small J. C. Penney's housed in a dull gray block of a building adjoining an auto parts store. Too, our little piece of supposed paradise turned out to be stuck somewhere circa 1950 with all the redneck, backwoods mentality to go with it. Even the single tiny diamond in Chan's ear evoked ridicule from his coworkers, driving him, finally, to take it out.

Alone at my desk facing the blank screen that was to be my novel, I found myself longing for a column like I'd had at the *Rocky*, this one to be centered on the Oregon coast. I wrote the editor at the *Oregonian* to plead my case. I told him how the coast was growing. I suggested stories that I,

The sun rises over Yaquina Bay.

living in the heart of the coast—Yaquina Bay on one side of town, the Pacific on the other—was uniquely positioned to write.

But the newspaper was cutting positions, not adding. And while I still held out hope in a Pollyannaish sort of way that the news business would rebound, the grim decline had been the story of my career, and it was getting harder and harder to foresee a bright future in the world of paper and ink.

So, I eked out a living freelancing, something I'd done most of my career. I landed a gig stringing for the *New York Times*. My first story was about Christian Longo, who murdered his wife and three children and threw their bodies in the Yaquina and Alsea Bays. It was only after I filed the story that I learned I would receive no byline. Weeks later, they sent in a correspondent for a more extensive story. He called with instructions on what I was to gather for him. When I balked, he noted I would be paid for my time, of course. It did not escape my attention that overnight I had gone from being a columnist and features writer at one of the largest metro papers in the country to being Girl Friday.

Mostly, I wrote magazine features and travel stories. I flew to Switzerland, Australia, Alaska, the Channel Islands of Jersey and Guernsey, usually first- or business-class, always staying in the best hotels, dining at the finest restaurants. It made for some memorable moments, and exposed me to experiences I talk about to this day—good and bad.

Once, flying back to Adelaide after a day of wine tasting and fine dining on the Fleurieu Peninsula, the woman next to me, Arlyn, nudged my shoulder. "What's the matter with the pilot?" she demanded in her Brooklyn accent.

"What do you mean what's the matter with the pilot?" I said.

"He's slumped over the wheel," she said.

I leaned forward, and sure enough, his body was draped over the controls. I had just one thought: there would be no new pilot getting on the plane to land us safely. It would be up to me, Arlyn, or the Chinese woman in the back, who had given herself the American moniker of Belinda Sunshine, to pilot the plane. I was utterly terror stricken. It was dark. We were flying over water. I did not have the kind of cool required to move into the pilot's seat and take instructions over the radio. I didn't even know how to use the radio. Those were the thoughts flying through my head as I leaned forward, grabbing the pilot by the shoulder. "What's the matter with you?" I demanded. Slowly, he rose from his "slumped" position, turned to me and said, "I was writing in my log by the light of the dash."

I sat back in my seat, waiting for my heart to slow. "See," Arlyn said. "I knew a girl who had lived in Alaska would know what to do." When we landed the pilot said I'd scared him so bad he almost wet himself. We tried to make up for it by handing over some of the swag Peninsula merchants had given us.

I also made some lifelong friends on those trips, including a former *Toronto Star* foreign correspondent who entertained me with stories from the war front, then listened politely while I read to him poems written by William Stafford. That was in the Switzerland town near the falls where Sir Arthur Conan Doyle killed off Sherlock Holmes, a bit of trivia everyone seemed to know but me.

I had the opportunity for experiences that would have otherwise never come my way: piloting a barge in the south of France; making fresh tracks on a ski slope in Vail with Warren Miller; sampling an octopus martini in Australia (no, I do not recommend it). But I got tired of being gone all the time, and Chan got lonely. One coworker teased that I was probably screwing around. Oh, the joys of small-town living.

The truth is, travel writing is not all it's cracked up to be. Sure, there are the premiere seats, best hotels, best food—and all on someone else's dime. But you pay in other ways. You're up early and at it all day and long into the night, every hour scheduled. Woe to the writer who should get sick or fail to show up for a scheduled event. Once, sick with a nasty stomach bug in New Orleans, I tried to bow out of a late evening meal. "Sorry," said the woman in charge of herding us around. "This is a command appearance." And appear I did.

A couple of years after my first note to the editor at the *Oregonian*, I wrote again. Within an hour of hitting "send," I found his reply. "I'd just been reading your story in *Portland Monthly* and wondering if you'd be interested in writing news for the *Oregonian*." Actually, I wasn't. Not news. News, as I recalled it from my early years as a general assignment reporter and then, capital bureau chief for a small eastern Connecticut daily, meant long hours in mind-numbing meetings, daily monitoring of police reports, long, drawn out courthouse hearings, and covering topics of which I had little interest or, worse, knowledge. It also meant working long hours for which there would often be no overtime pay—a pattern that I saw repeatedly in the business.

But writing news for the *Oregonian* would mean a regular paycheck and "no" didn't feel like an option. And I would not be on staff, but a stringer, a correspondent, charged with covering an area from Florence to Astoria, roughly one-third of the coast. That I would be a correspondent was both good and bad. On one hand, I would still largely be able to call my days my own (or so I naively imagined), but I would not have any benefits. I also knew some people tended to regard stringers as something like the B league. As one local put it, "Oh, but you're just a stringer, aren't you?"

I interviewed in Portland at the old stone building on Broadway. Even then, it was a forlorn gray kind of place that I could not help but compare to the polished stone of the *Rocky*. Still, this was my one hope of working for a real newspaper again, for being a part of things—in my own re-moved sort of way.

The editor asked what my goal for the job would be. "I want to own the coast," I said. I met with three different editors and later joined two report-ers for coffee across the street. I guessed it was their job to see if I would be a good fit and report back to the editor in charge of hiring me. When it came up that I'd gone to school in Philly as a teen, and my colleague guessed I must have attended classes at Temple University, I couldn't bring myself to correct him: that I had attended John Robert Powers modeling school on Saturdays. And when that same colleague complimented me on my clips, saying he'd read every one of them top to bottom, something he admitted he never did, I took it as the compliment intended, but imme-diately found myself fighting back dread. All of my clips were features or first-person pieces. Did I even know how to write news anymore?

There were also rumors about the *Oregonian's* treatment of correspon-dents. Once in a conversation with a features editor, she whispered, "Are you sure you want to do this? I've talked with other correspondents and the editors work their asses off."

I got the job offer on St. Patrick's Day. My first story would be about a model ship builder in North Bend—oh, about sixty miles south of the area we agreed I'd cover. It was an apt beginning. In short time, I'd be covering all 360-odd miles of the Oregon coast.

Stringing lasted a year and a half before the *Oregonian* brought a few of us on board as staff writers—albeit part-time. First, we were hired for thirty hours a week, then after the Affordable Care Act, we were cut back to twenty-eight. My passion has always been in fiction. At the *Oregonian*, that was my timecard. But often as not, I chose to work the extra hours, because when it came down to it, either I did the story or someone else would.

Despite my early misgivings, I came quickly to believe that I had been blessed with the best writing gig on Earth—albeit a dark one. I was always racing somewhere, and it was rarely for anything good. Often it involved death. Car crashes. Falls. Murders. Suicide. Murder and suicide. Drownings. Capsizings. God, there were a lot of capsizings. I don't think I'll ever be able to look out over that winter ocean, see the city of lights that is the crab fleet, and not worry, not feel that squeeze in my gut and wonder not if, but when.

In the midst of it all, I dealt with my own personal tragedy. The loss of my dad, a once handsome, lean, muscled man who back in the day kept his Lucky Strikes rolled in the sleeve of his T-shirt and sported a six pack that came from hard work, coupled with the fact that he'd lost part of his stomach after taking a bullet in Korea. My dad was the storyteller in our family, and I like to think my love of a good tale grew from him.

Seven years after I stood beside my father as he gasped his final breaths, I learned of the loss of my mother. I've come to believe her letters to my brother in Vietnam and her morning notes, written to me and my sister before she left for work, were likely my earliest inspiration to write. News of her death came early one summer day as I stood on the beach covering one of the biggest stories of the year.

Working on the Oregon coast made me a better writer and a better person, but it also made me wary, tentative, watchful: I don't run on the beach without knowing the tide; I don't ever step beyond the signs that warn not to—I don't even get close; and the sound of a sharp bang is never just a backfire, but a potential murder, suicide, or both. I'm sure I've always had some of that wariness in me, but covering the Oregon coast amplified it many times over.

Nonetheless, if many of the mileposts along Highway 101 are defined for me by someone else's tragedy, so too are they reminders that I am blessed with having the privilege of working in the most amazing setting, a place where life is authentic and the landscape so stunningly beautiful, all these years later, it can still take my breath away.

I always said there was a book in this beat.

And so, here are the stories behind the stories, the personal losses, the tales that are in my blood and bones, and sometimes haunt me in the middle of the night—including teens Jenny and Kara, who I promise I will not forget.

ONE

IF SOMEONE DIES

2004

I had been writing for the *Oregonian* for about three months when the entire volunteer fire department walked off the job in Wheeler, a little town set on the hillside above Nehalem Bay on the north coast. By then, I'd written about a veterinarian whose practice doubled as the animal shelter; as such she had euthanized more than thirteen hundred stray dogs and cats in her thirteen years in Tillamook. After hearing her practice referred to as the slaughterhouse, she was closing up shop and leaving town.

I'd written about a house in Astoria threatening to collapse on itself after an excavating job below compromised the hillside on which it sat, and about a Clatsop County human resources director who was hanging up his coat and tie for a military uniform and tour in Afghanistan. He and his wife prepared by drawing up his will.

I was learning, and I had plenty more to learn.

I wasn't used to writing nut graphs—a paragraph near the top of a story that explains what the story is about—and resisted them, which was futile. To me, nut graphs that give away the end are the epitome of bad story telling. Why read a story through to the end when the writer has already divulged the outcome up top? I also had to learn what a story was by the *Oregonian*'s standards, and I often pitched ideas that I supposed must have seemed kind of laughable. Like the Wheeler story. The volunteer firemen had walked off the job in support of their chief, who by day was the public works director. I called my editor to ask if it was a story for us.

"If someone dies, then it's a story, Lori," he said.

"Oh, right," I said. I knew what he meant was if there was a fire, and someone died because there were no firemen to fight it, that was a story. But a bunch of volunteers walking off the job in a little bitty town was not. I hung up feeling embarrassed for even suggesting it. I moved on to the next story on my list, which happened to be the one-year anniversary of the *Taki-Tooo*, a charter boat that flipped on the Tillamook Bay bar in Garibaldi in June 2003. Eleven people, including the skipper, died in the Father's Day tragedy. Eight survived.

When the *Taki-Tooo* tragedy occurred the year before, I had the firm sense that I needed to do something, but I didn't know exactly what that was. While I had resisted the idea of being a "news" reporter, years of being in newsrooms had ingrained in me a sense of needing to go to work when a story broke.

I had been in the newsroom in 1987, an intern of sorts at the Reading Eagle, when Pennsylvania Treasurer Budd Dwyer, accused of accepting a bribe, had put a gun in his mouth in the middle of a live TV news conference and ended his life. In an instant, the newsroom hummed with an energy I'd never before encountered. Every reporter, every editor, every single soul stopped what he or she was doing and became part of the effort. I was both fascinated and overwhelmed, intimidated at the thought that I would have to play a part, relieved when I did not.

Over the years, I've come to realize that in writing, photographing, reporting, you have a task: to get the story, get it right, and make deadline. That task, not necessarily the news on which it is centered, becomes the focus. It gives you something specific to do in a dark hour when there is nothing more you can do. Of course, there will be plenty of time later for the horror of what has unfolded to sink in.

But my work for the *New York Times* had dried up the year the *Taki-Tooo* capsized. I had no news market to write for. I had no task to complete. And so, I'd watched and listened from afar as the death count was tallied and retallied, as the TV crews and newspaper reporters and broadcast journalists took over Garibaldi. Now here I was one year later, charged with writing the anniversary story. So many had covered that story and covered it well. What could I bring to the table that others had not?

Garibaldi is a tiny town set on Tillamook Bay, marked on its hillside by

A fishing vessel heads out to sea.

an oversized white G. There are a handful of shops, mostly secondhand and antique, a few bars, restaurants and grocery stores, a hotel, motel and RV park, and a stately white building—recognizable up and down the coast as a US Coast Guard station. Garibaldi bills itself as Oregon's "Authentic Fishing Village." It's true enough, but just as true many other places on the Oregon coast.

Boats dock on the bay, then motor north to cross the bar—that place where the mighty waters of the Pacific collide with the relative calm of the bay. Many coastal harbors in Oregon have jetties built out of boulders, some the size of small cars, extending out into the water to help boats navigate safely from the harbor to the sea.

The force of the waters, combined with unpredictable waves, wind, and sediment deposits that can make the channels shallow all contribute to hazardous bar crossings. And while the best time to cross any bar depends on conditions, it is generally held that crossing at flood tide is safest because the water is deeper and the waves smaller.

In any case, if a boat is going to go down, odds are it will happen on the bar. And odds are, any number of people will be out by the jetty watching. Here, as in many other places on the coast, locals make it part of their daily routine to drive to the jetty, where every seat is front row and where a scattering of crosses bear witness to the bar crossings that did not end well.

In Garibaldi, I stopped first at Garibaldi Charters, which had owned the *Taki-Tooo*. A young woman at the desk said I'd probably find owner Mick Buell at the docks. So on I drove, and sure enough, there he was tinkering around on one of his boats on "charter row." I introduced myself and braced for his response. He had lost his friend Captain Doug Davis and nearly lost his daughter. As the boat owner, he had suffered scathing criticisms, accusations, and blame. I imagined the last thing he wanted to do was revisit a capsizing that would go down in history as one of the deadliest marine tragedies in Oregon's history. In fact, he couldn't have been kinder, though he didn't have a lot to say.

The next stop was the Port of Garibaldi. I found a restaurant and took a barstool in a lounge with stained brown carpet and faded decor. This was the part I dreaded. The part where I introduced myself to strangers and hoped they might be willing to talk, might have something to add to my story, hoped at the very least they wouldn't growl at me and mutter something rude about the media.

On this afternoon, there was only me, a waitress/bartender, who hadn't been around the year before, and one other customer in the place. I summoned my nerve and introduced myself. He gestured to the empty seat opposite him. I pulled out the chair and opened my notebook.

Earl Wernecke Jr. was on the jetty that morning. It was just before 7:00 a.m. Four charter boats idled on the bay, waiting their turn.

First up was the *Norwester*. It rode one swell, then caught a second and stood up on end. It recovered and motored on. Next came the *Oakland Pilot*. It hit a swell and plummeted ten feet, smacking the water so violently the deckhand was knocked unconscious. Only the *D&D* made it across unscathed. Each skipper warned by radio of debris, mainly logs, littering the water.

Then it was the *Taki-Tooo*'s turn. Wernecke grew so unnerved watching, he had to turn away. That's when he heard Buell yell, "The boat went over. Help me!"

On that morning, Buell had gone to the north jetty to watch the boats cross the bar. In addition to the *Taki-Tooo*, Buell and his wife, Linda, also owned the *D&D* and the *Norwester*. If the vessels made it across safely, Buell would go about his day. But if any of the captains deemed the bar too rough and turned back, Buell would rush to the charter office to refund the clients' money.

That afternoon, a year later, Wernecke talked in a voice still shaken. He talked about the bodies, about seeing his girlfriend try to revive a man with mouth-to-mouth resuscitation, and realizing the man's neck was broken. He told me about the man he carried in from the surf, his face blue, his eyes wide.

"It's the same picture in my sleep every night," he said. "It keeps me awake."

I wrote it all down in my slender white notebook with the *Oregonian* inked on the cover and a place below for the reporter's name and date. When he finished, I thanked him and went back to my hotel room. It was only then that I realized how naive I had been. How stupid. For all I knew, Wernecke had read the same stories I had, had seen the same TV reports and repeated it all for me. How did I know I could trust him? I didn't. It was another one of those moments when I felt like an amateur, when I knew a "real" news reporter would have thought of that and dealt with it in the first place.

Down in the hotel lobby, I stopped by the front desk and told the clerk what I was up to.

"Four of the men who died were staying here," she said. "It was so sad. They were so happy to be here. They were having such a good time."

We stood quietly for a moment. Four men I didn't know were dead. Four men who had laughed and goofed off right here in this lobby. Gone. We both sighed, and I said I supposed I'd better get myself some dinner, and headed out across the street to the pub, where I found mostly men drinking and watching TV. I ordered dinner to go and a glass of wine, and struck up a conversation with the man next to me. He was a bearded guy with a gut that spilled over a belt that did nothing to keep his pants up. I told him why I was in town.

"Oh, not this again," he said. "Why can't you media people just leave it alone? You don't need to start this again. You know, the last time you reporters came to town, we couldn't pay people to come here and fish. Nobody would go out on the charters. Business is still down. People here are hurting. They don't want a story. We don't want to be in the news."

I knew what he said was true. That morning on "charter row," Buell had told me business was down 25 percent since the capsizing. Another charter operator told me they'd taken out only ninety people since the season opened in May. Before the *Taki-Tooo*, they would have hauled that many in three days.

I made a lame attempt to explain myself to the man at the bar, but it was pointless. And so we sat in silence, he clearly pissed off and me wondering if I should leave before it got worse. But there was the waitress speeding toward me with my brown-bagged dinner. I gulped back the last of my wine, and as I slipped out the door, you could almost hear the room echo, "Good riddance." It shouldn't have mattered, but it did. They were just small-town people trying to make a living like the rest of us. But eleven people had died. Eleven people who thought they were going out to sea for a day of fun on Father's Day. How many of them knew how dangerous the Tillamook Bay bar can be? How many ever considered that in their quest for fish and fun they might die instead? If we didn't tell the stories, remind people that bad things do happen even during what are supposed to be the best of times, who would? Still, I felt a bit like a vulture. This would no doubt be a cover story with my byline, which is what most print journalists aimed for. People were more likely to read it, and writers write to be read. And yet there was no denying it would come at the expense of many who had already felt enough pain.

The next day on my way home, I stopped at a little Laundromat in Tillamook where I found Mick Buell's daughter, Tamara. A slender girl with a rope of hair trailing down her back, sectioned off in bands of bright color, she was quiet, polite. She had been a deckhand on the *Taki-Tooo*, one of eight people who came out of the ocean alive. A surfer, snowboarder, and rugby player, she liked life with a certain edge to it. Just twenty-two at the time of the tragedy, she'd still had some of the invincibility that comes with youth. As the wave raced toward the fishing vessel, she yelled for everyone to take off their rain gear, then moments later found herself choking on the diesel-fouled water as the dead floated by. She knew she was going to die.

That day, as we sat side by side on the bench opposite the dryers at the Laundromat her family owned, she told me, "It would have been so much easier to stop swimming." Her voice wavered, her eyes brimmed with tears. "That's when I got mad," she said. "I didn't want to go yet."

Moments later, her foot found a sand bar, and the ocean gave up its hold.

Back home in my office, I pulled up the old clips of the *Taki-Tooo* from my colleagues the year before—something (ahem) I most surely should have done before embarking on my little witness-finding mission. And sure enough, there was Earl Wernecke Jr. in black and white with his eye-witness account from the jetty—just like he'd told me in the lounge.

Next, I reached out to Mark Hamlett, one of the survivors from the wreck. Unlike those in Garibaldi who did not want the story resurrected, Hamlett, a contractor and recreational boat operator himself, was more than willing to share his story, a reminder to the world of how quickly the good times turn bad. There wasn't a day he didn't relive the nightmare, and he went over it with me patiently—as often as needed—so that I could recreate those moments. He had strong opinions about what had gone wrong, and he had no qualms about sharing them. Hamlett had boarded the *Taki-Tooo* with both his sons, Daniel and Christopher, his son-in-law, Brian Loll, and Brian's Dad, Ed Loll. Ed and his wife were visiting from Iowa. Ed Loll had never been on the Pacific Ocean before. He was one of the eleven who didn't make it off the charter boat alive. Hamlett didn't expect to.

"When we were looking at the third wave," Hamlett recalled, "I said, 'My wife and my daughter have just lost their entire family.' It was the most devastating thought I've ever had."

Hamlett believes skipper Doug Davis lost his nerve, plunging ahead when he should have waited, then turning the boat sideways to the wave.

I filed my story on the *Taki-Tooo* on a Friday. That evening, Chan came home from his monthly union meeting complaining he didn't feel well. Something about his stomach. When he refused a beer, I knew he really didn't feel well. I asked where it hurt? He said, all over. I figured he'd picked up some benign bug on his recent flight to Colorado for his annual rafting trip with the guys.

In the morning when we awoke, Chan still didn't feel well. I asked again where it hurt, and he placed his hand over the lower part of his stomach. He was hurting bad but, like he usually did, was trying to downplay it. Chan, all six feet, six inches, and 240-ish pounds of him, is mortally afraid of needles. He traces this to the day in school when the girl in line ahead of him got a vaccination, fainted, and crashed to the floor. But almost worse than Chan's fear of needles was the grim advice we'd heard repeatedly from the day we moved here: if you're sick, go to the valley. That meant Corvallis—a good hour-plus drive away.

"I think you better take me to the emergency room," Chan said. We were still just awakening, but now looking at him I saw that the whites of his eyes were yellow. Yellow! We pulled on our clothes and raced the six or so miles to the local hospital, but outside the ER doors, Chan stopped. "Let's go to the valley."

"You don't have time," I said, pushing him through the door. The registering nurse took one look at him, called for a stretcher, and that quick they wheeled him off. I was left to do the paperwork and worry. When I finished, they escorted me to a space in the back where Chan awaited laid out in his hospital gown. A male nurse asked if he'd ever had a problem with his appendix before.

Chan and I looked at each other and nodded, grinning a little at the memory of our first summer together in Anchorage. It was a Sunday. He'd been sick and in pain for several days. But not so sick we couldn't enjoy a little morning romp—or so I thought. He didn't tell me until much after the deed was done that he thought he was going to die from the pain. But at least it got him serious about getting to the ER. There, they diagnosed him with an infected appendix and sent him home with antibiotics. For twenty-three years his appendix never made another peep. Now the reprieve was up. The nurse was European and said not operating immediately was typical treatment in his home country, but very progressive for the United States, especially all those years ago.

While we waited for the surgeon, I rushed home to feed our three dogs, promising Chan I'd be right back, but when I returned barely thirty minutes later, he was on his way to surgery. I panicked. They had to let me see him first. They raced me up to the room, but he was already out of it.

I made my way back to the waiting room, then spotted through the glass door a small courtyard labyrinth. I went outside and began to walk it. The irony was inescapable. I'd spent the week coaxing people to talk about death, and now here it was on my doorstep. And all the while, the same thoughts played over and over. What if it wasn't his appendix? What if it was something worse? Like cancer? What if he died? This is what I do in life. What if? It seems death is always just around the corner. And it always has been. Maybe it was the sudden loss of my beloved uncle, who'd gone home after our Christmas celebration and inexplicably died. Or three years later, at the age of eight, seeing my father's friend killed in a race car crash.

Whatever the cause, I always expect the worst.

I walked the labyrinth for another ten minutes, then went back inside, where the nurse found me still pacing.

"I saw you outside walking, and I know you're worried," he said. "It was his appendix. He was lucky. It was gangrenous and four times its normal size, but they got it. He should be fine."

My cell phone rang. I excused myself and went outside. It was the copy desk: was this a good time to go over edits on the *Taki-Tooo* story?

When my editor called in July, he explained he wasn't too sure exactly what bar pilots do, but apparently there was trouble brewing between the pilots and the agency that paid them. I connected with the Columbia River Bar Pilots in Astoria by phone and found they were not only happy to explain to me what they did, they wanted to show me. I packed a bag, booked a hotel room, and zoomed off for Astoria—about a three-hour drive if you don't get stuck behind one of the leisurely visitors who don't understand the purpose of highway pull outs.

At the hangar, I found a welcoming crew, eager to share details of their demanding job. They were set to fly out to meet a ship just beyond the Columbia River Bar in a short time and wanted me to go along with them. I'd get to experience their work as closely as possible without actually doing it. Then they told me that in order to do so, I would have to undergo certain steps required by the FAA (Federal Aviation Administration) and that included rappelling out of the helicopter—just the way the bar pilots do. It made no sense to me. I'd flown in helos before and hadn't had to prove anything more than the ability to buckle my seatbelt. But they insisted this was the only way. I agreed, and instantly felt my guts tumble in dread.

Phobias are strange afflictions. Often inexplicable. Irrational. Occasionally crippling. I have two. One of them is snakes; the other, heights.

I am the woman at the top of the skyscraper refusing to take in the view. I discovered my fear in my late twenties after climbing a fire tower in the Berkshires of Massachusetts. Reaching the top for a look at the vibrant fall foliage below, I suddenly panicked, and nearly paralyzed with fear, could not move. My husband finally got me down by sitting me on my butt and coaxing me one step at a time to the bottom. It was not a lesson I needed to learn twice, but the unavoidable, unforeseeable times I have found myself way the hell up there, I have reacted in the same irrational, unfathomable manner. My heart pounds, my body trembles, and putting one foot in front of the other is akin to an impending dance of death.

And so there I was in the hangar, a story to be written, and the best, maybe only way to write it was to dangle from a helicopter as it hovered over the Astoria Airport parking lot.

The mechanic put me through the motions, including using the harness I would wear to rappel, his eyes ever on the clock as the hour of our rendezvous with the incoming cargo ship grew closer. Finished, we met with the rest of the crew and headed out to the helicopter.

The pilot lifted us up into the air. I slipped on the harness. The hoist operator/mechanic clipped me into the rigging inside the helo and helped me to the door. Facing what might as well have been the Grand Canyon, I was utterly terrified. There was just no possible way I could step out into the abyss.

I lowered myself to my butt.

"Go ahead, you'll be fine," someone said. "We don't have much time."

And so I did what I do when I am terrified and seem to have no choice: I jumped. In this case, it was more like scooting, but there I was dangling in midair high above the ground. Soon, however, before I'd had time to even panic, the asphalt was growing closer. It wasn't so bad, after all. And then, just like that, I'd done it. Now, feet planted, I followed the training instructions. I unhooked from the line tethering me to the helo, showed my hands, then clipped back in, heeding, I thought, their warnings that if my harness wasn't adjusted right I might start swinging. You know, like a pendulum. I had no intention of letting that happen. Slowly, I rose from the ground. But now terra firma was growing ever distant, and I was beyond terror stricken. Then, I started swirling. I clenched my jaw, pain shooting up the side of my head like an electric shock, but in that moment all I knew was that I had to get inside that damned helicopter. I was probably still a good foot from the door when I started reaching for it.

I crawled in on all fours, the sense of relief so great I could have cried. The guys, on the other hand, were laughing like I was just the best entertainment they'd seen in a long time. "I thought you were going to climb right up that line," one of them said. More laughter. I forced a smile. Right, just fucking hysterical. Hours later, my jaw still ached.

But now it was time to go to work for real. The Columbia River Bar is one of the most dangerous in the world, certainly in Oregon, and part of a body of water dubbed the "Graveyard of the Pacific." The bar stretches three miles wide between Oregon and Washington and is six miles long. According to the Columbia River Bar Pilots website, foreign vessels engaged in trade are required to hire a Columbia River Bar Pilot licensed by the state of Oregon when crossing the bar. Each pilot must hold an unlimited master's license and have served at least two years as master on oceangoing vessels.

On board, the pilot takes control of the ship, navigating it over the bar of the Columbia River to and from sea. Bar pilots guide approximately 3,600 ships: from 100-foot tugs to 1,100-foot tankers as well as bulk carriers, car carriers, log ships, general cargo ships, container ships, and passenger ships each year.

I was about to get a bird's-eye view of exactly how it works.

We flew to the mouth of the Columbia River, where a massive container ship sat waiting. The bar pilot slipped into the harness and the hoist operator lowered him to the ship deck, where he unhooked from the harness and disappeared to do his job. Later, the helicopter would return to lift him from the ship. We flew back to the airport and talked about how I might approach the story. In addition to flying out to meet the cargo ships, the bar pilots also board the ships via their own multimillion dollar custom-built boat.

The boat sidles up close to the massive ships, allowing the bar pilot to grasp a rope ladder and climb to the deck. One of the pilots suggested someday I might try boarding a ship from the boat. Wow, I thought, what a story that could be. And honestly, having just faced down one of my biggest fears, I considered giving it a try. So I began pondering how I might actually climb the side of a ship the size of a small skyscraper without falling to my death. (This also came up a summer later when I was invited to Antarctica with some scientists who would have to board a research ship from a small raft. "If you fall in, you will die," one of them advised. They never followed up on the invitation. Neither did I.)

I agreed to meet with the bar pilot crew in the morning for breakfast and a ride on their boat, then another trip aboard the helo. I checked into my hotel room and called my editor to tell him about my day, my thoughts on the story, and the possibility of boarding the ship with one of the pilots. He laughed. "Be careful, Lori. I don't think our insurance will cover you." He was right. As a correspondent, I had no medical coverage, and since I was working under contract, I assumed I wouldn't be eligible for worker's comp. Still, I had a story to write and these were the details, the up-close experiences that made for good stories.

It was just after midnight when I awoke with spins the like of which I had never known. I was not just dizzy, but off balance, unmoored to the point of incomprehension. When I turned my head, the room orbited around me, not in any kind of rhythm I could at least feebly grasp, but in a cruel sort of Tilt-a-Whirl that sent me lurching from wall to wall. Alone in the dark, I worked my way to the bathroom, then sitting, nearly fell off the toilet. Somehow, I made it back to bed where I stayed perfectly still until somehow I fell back asleep. I awoke periodically through the night scared half to death, praying in the morning it would be gone. But when I climbed out of bed, it was just as bad. I'd had some red wine the night before. Maybe I'd drunk more than I realized? It was the only thing that made sense, except I knew I hadn't drank that much.

By the time I met the pilots for breakfast, the symptoms had subsided somewhat, and by doing everything very slowly, gripping whatever was nearby for support, I was able to pretend some sort of normalcy. I got through the meal, but I worried how I was going to handle a boat ride on the Columbia River and then another ride on the helicopter, this time to retrieve a bar pilot from the deck of a ship. But as it turned out, I was fine. The boat, at that time it was the Chinook, looked every inch of its $3.3 million price tag with leather and wood interior befitting a yacht, and when it was time for my second helicopter ride, I got to stay inside.

On the way home, I stopped by Camp Meriwether, the Cascade Pacific Boy Scout Council's oldest summer camp, where I'd been invited to write a feature story about all the good going on there. I joined them for a meal, standing in the full dining hall with the boys as they said grace, then sat, carefully serving themselves a small portion, then passing the bowl to the next boy, taking seconds only after all had been served. Once the meal was over, the boys listened as the leaders gave instructions for the afternoon, then excused themselves to return to their adventures outside. The inner child in me felt a wee bit of envy, not only for the idyllic setting the boys could call their own, but also for the order, the certainty of their days. Later, I would learn that only a year before a young man had died after lighting a cannon and making the tragic mistake of looking inside when it initially failed to go off. My originally conceived feel-good story would become a balancing act between writing around the one-year anniversary news peg, as my editors decreed, and honoring the trust of the Boy Scout leaders who had opened their camp to me. Such stories were never an easy walk.

After day number two on the road, I finally pulled into my driveway at about five. I was feeling okay, but still uneasy. The dizziness was gone, but I sensed it lingering on the periphery.

When I got up the next morning, and it hit me all over again, I knew something was terribly, terribly wrong. My family doctor agreed to see me right away. In his office, I explained the situation, expecting an emergency visit to the hospital for tests. Instead, the doctor looked at me, crossed his arms over his chest, and said, "You have benign positional vertigo."

I wanted to believe him. Such a simple explanation for something so incapacitating. Could it be?

Days later, the ear specialist confirmed the diagnosis and told me that benign positional vertigo is the most common inner ear condition causing dizziness. I researched it on the Internet and learned that I should sleep sitting partially up, and avoid turning my head to the bad side, my left, when lying flat on my back. I learned on my own that it was also a bad idea to tilt my head skyward. The good news was that it would eventually pass or at least calm. The bad—it would likely return, perhaps for the rest of my life, with little or no warning. To this day, I never sleep on my back without a minimum of two pillows. In the gym, I have learned new ways of working my abs without lying flat for crunches, and when faced with adjusting something overhead, I tend to do so semi-blindly, glancing up only momentarily.

A few weeks after I was diagnosed, I watched a documentary in which a helicopter rescued a man from floodwaters. As he was rising into the sky, the narrator warned, "They have to be very careful now or he could start spinning and develop vertigo." And so, I had my answer. It had not been the red wine or an oncoming cold or pure bad luck, but the spinning, no doubt made all the worse by the panicked clenching of my jaw.

That summer when I rappelled for the first and, trust me, last time, I never did write about the bar pilots. Instead, they settled their pay dispute with the shippers' association, and my hope of writing a feature on them died when I learned another writer had done the same just two years prior.

A little more than a year later on a stormy night with the seas swelling to twenty feet, a new bar pilot jumped from the rope ladder aside a 558-foot-long log carrier to the awaiting Chinook. Just as he leapt, the seas pitched the Chinook, the pilot missed the landing and fell into the churning Columbia River. Despite the immediate efforts to reach him, he was carried away. They recovered the body two nights later.

In September 2004 I had been living on the coast for four years, but I'd never been to Manzanita except to blow past it while racing up to Cannon Beach or Seaside or Astoria. Manzanita is an oceanfront village of old cottages and new condos. At the time the community liked to think of itself as undiscovered—though it would be years before I learned this and not in the friendliest of ways. I also didn't know that it was perhaps the most dog-friendly place on the coast: the place where the pub welcomes dogs into its beer garden, the espresso shop sells dog dishes, and a yellow caution sign depicts a dog reminding motorists to slow down. But one day it was not so friendly anymore. Someone was poisoning dogs.

Between August 11 and September 5, ten dogs died, all after recent visits to the beach. Police feared someone was seeding the beach with paraquat, a toxic chemical used in landscaping to kill weeds and grass. Only one death was confirmed a poisoning, but the other nine were highly suspicious. Paraquat passes through the system quickly, and many people had waited too long to have their dogs tested or had not realized the possibility of poisoning and had simply buried their best friend.

The same thing had happened the year before in Portland's Laurelhurst Park. There, sixteen dogs died after eating sausage or other meat spiked with the poison. But in Manzanita police could find no evidence of how the dogs were getting the paraquat. I called a Portland veterinarian clinic to discuss the possibility that poisonings here on the coast were linked to those in Portland. The spokesperson downplayed the possibility of a connection, but instead suggested that since paraquat was used in landscaping, perhaps there was an accidental spill? Perhaps it had been carried in by birds? The possibilities were vast, she said. Better accidental than intentional, I thought. After September 5, no more dogs were poisoned, and Manzanita was again a safe place for a romp on the beach.

And so I'd discovered Manzanita, and fell in love. It became the place Chan and I spent New Year's Eve and participated in the midnight parade from the pub to the beach, the place where we celebrated birthdays and sometimes traveled just to escape everyday life, always taking the pups with us. We stayed at a reasonably priced oceanfront motel that didn't bitch if we snuck off to the pub for a quick one and left the pups behind. It had a swimming pool, unparalleled views, and a colander in the kitchen cabinet, which always made me long to cook spaghetti, though it was really meant for cleaning crab. Manzanita and the motel became what felt like the closest thing we'd know to a second home, and yet in the years to come, the village became the place of more darkness than any other place on the coast—a darkness that would come to feel incredibly personal and as strange as any story I know.

In the months since I'd learned about the missing fire department radio, I had forgotten about the volunteer firefighters and the troubles in Wheeler, which happens to be just down the hill and around the curve from Manzanita. Then one day I found myself reading a mysteriously mournful op-ed in the *Tillamook Headlight Herald*. All I could make sense of the piece was that it was somehow connected to the firefighters, who'd earlier that year walked off the job in support of public works director/volunteer fire chief Ken Painter. After a showdown with some local kids over a missing piece of equipment, the new town manager had booted him from his city job. The town was beyond divided. People were enraged.

I recalled the conversation with my editor in March about the firefighters, and his comment, "If someone dies, then it's a story." And now, here was an editorial underscored with grief and regret, and clearly linked to the ongoing skirmish between the firefighters and the town manager. But how? What?

Months earlier, I had met a reporter from the *Headlight Herald* while covering the trial of Edward Morris. Morris is the guy who, four days before Christmas in 2002, drove his family to Tillamook with the promise of spending some time at the coast. He then parked at a wayside, told his wife he had a surprise for her, and shot her in the face. He shot each of his two sons as they awoke, then drove to the Tillamook forest and stuck a knife in his daughter eighteen times, maybe more. The murders came just one year after Christian Longo murdered his family.

Now, I picked up the phone and dialed the Tillamook reporter. Someone had indeed died. It was time for the story.

On a sunny day, I drove two hours north to Wheeler, population about four hundred. Sitting across from Nehalem Bay, Wheeler has an idyllic setting, but it also has a worn, faded feel, even with its gussied up hotel and antique shops. (On another assignment, I'd spend a morning with the Tillamook bookmobile and discover the part of Wheeler locals know—the pretty, old houses set high on the hillside gazing over the bay and forest—and be glad this little place remains a secret to at least some.)

Wheeler is a town more easily defined by what it is not than what it is. It is not, for example, Manzanita to the north, with beachfront and homes tending to the high six figures to $1 million range. And it's not Tillamook to the south, where it frequently floods in the winter and often smells like cow poop.

That morning, I parked on a side street and took a walk, looking for the kind of people who seemed least likely to snarl when I announced, "Hi, I'm Lori Tobias with the *Oregonian*." I was slowly growing accustomed to this necessary engagement of perfect strangers, but it was still awkward for me—encounters such as the one in the Garibaldi pub were still fresh. It's not that people were frequently unkind, but when they were, it smarted. It felt personal, undeserved, and just plain mean. As near as I could figure out, a rude response generally stemmed from the fact that I was (a) an outsider, (b) a reporter, and (c) most importantly, a reporter from the outside. Of course, it didn't help that I was usually on the scene to talk about something most people would have preferred I forgot.

I spoke first with Willow Bill, a gentle soul who made furniture out of willow branches and was saddened by his divided community, but not surprised. It seemed Wheeler had something of a history of that. I sat for a moment with a cashier at a small gift shop, who also knew the various players in the battle between city manager Gene Norris and Painter. She also was at a loss to explain, though she seemed genuinely fond of at least one of the teens involved. Then, I took a seat on a sidewalk bench and waited to see who else might appear. On a fall weekday in Wheeler you could sit a long time without bumping in to anyone, but eventually a man in a sporty little car showed up. He looked like he'd probably migrated from California. In a town where the dress code is tie dye and torn jeans, and travel is by pickup truck, the pricey car, dress slacks, and button-down made it clear he might have been in Wheeler, but he was not of Wheeler. I told him why I was in town. He waved a hand through the air and rolled his eyes. He had more important concerns, like the fact that the city wouldn't allow signs on Wheeler sidewalks so businesses could attract passers-by. Soon, the woman from the gift shop joined us. They greeted each other, friendly enough. But moments later when she offered a comment on our conversation, California erupted: "Goddamn it, don't interrupt me." For a moment she and I froze, then she shrugged, rolled her eyes and walked off, and California resumed his complaints about city hall and signage.

I had an appointment with Chuck, a city councilor who cautioned if I approached his street from the north, I would have to make a dangerous left-hand turn to his house and wouldn't I please drive past, then circle back to make a safer right-hand turn. Up the steep hill, I pulled into the drive of a house adorned with prayer flags and found Chuck waiting on the other side of the screen door. We sat down at his kitchen table where he related his version of things. When he finished, he told me:

"Gene was a fine man; Ken was as indispensable as an employee could be. This is really a tragedy. It makes me want to weep."

Back in my office, I made a half a dozen more calls until finally I had what I thought was the full story.

In June, someone had stolen the fire department's emergency radio from Painter's truck. It wasn't long before he got a tip that it was a couple of local kids looking to make money selling it. Painter went to the apartment where the kids hung out and allegedly threatened to kick their collective asses. The kids—ranging in ages from about twelve to twenty—cried to their parents; the parents complained and threatened to sue. Meanwhile, Painter swore that all he'd done was plead to get his radio back.

Norris, seventy, had been the city manager for all of four months. Before moving to the coast he'd lived in Portland, where I'm told he owned an auto repair shop. He had no prior experience in running a little town, but everyone knew him for his various civic duties and everyone, it seemed, liked him. He was even named volunteer of the year.

Wheeler had been through three city managers in three years. There was constant squabbling and tension among city councilmen, one who described the town as "an odd mix of Wild West mentality and good old boy politics." In Norris, locals saw a man who could calm things, bring people together. They offered him the job with a salary of $37,000 a year, and Norris said yes. "He was doing the town a favor," his friend told me.

Now he was faced with a lawsuit, maybe more than one. The city attorney was on vacation, so he called the fill-in, who suggested he call the insurance company attorneys. You don't have to be a psychic to know that once the insurance company got involved, things were going to go to hell fast. So, despite Painter's insistence of his innocence, despite his long service to the city, Norris did as he was directed and put Painter on paid administrative leave. That's when the fire crew turned in their pagers. There were verbal attacks and nasty letters. And arrests.

For his efforts to find the city's $850 emergency radio—which, in a city with an annual budget of only $615,000 was going to be damned hard to replace—Painter faced felony and misdemeanor charges, potentially a prison sentence, and extensive fines.

One hundred and fifty people signed a petition to get Painter reinstated, but in August, citing insubordination, Norris fired him. The verbal and written attacks grew so ugly, Norris feared being alone in the office, his wife told me. Eventually the stress landed him in the hospital, and in late August, he finally took his friends' advice and resigned.

Painter's first hearing on the appeal of his termination went before city council in September, but Norris couldn't bring himself to attend. The appeal was continued. On September 29, one day before Painter was due before the city council, Norris's wife found her husband dead of a self-inflicted gunshot wound.

Nearly a year passed before Painter's case finally went to trial. It lasted most of the day. His family was there to show their support. Whatever worries they harbored, they hid them well. But surely underneath that positive show of solidarity, they had to be worried. There was the possibility of prison and steep fines. He'd already lost his job and spent a year and a half defending his family's name. All for trying to retrieve a stolen emergency radio. The trial might have been laughable if the consequences had not been so damning.

Thomas White, one of the primary witnesses for the prosecution, told police that Painter came to his apartment and threatened to break his legs. Beau Golightly, a fire cadet who shared White's apartment, collaborated his story, as did a twelve-year-old girl and White's teenaged girlfriend. On the stand, Golightly, now a father, admitted he'd lied to investigators about Painter on several occasions. The girlfriend changed her testimony three times, finally admitting she couldn't remember what had happened.

"If you don't believe the state's witnesses, we're done," Tillamook County Chief Deputy District Attorney Brian Erickson told jurors in closing arguments.

It took the ten-man, two-woman jury less than a half an hour to acquit Painter on all charges. It happened so fast they had to send out a search party for the judge who'd slipped out for dinner.

In the end, one man lost his life, another his job, and Wheeler lost its volunteer fire department. As for the $850 radio, it was later returned anonymously.

In mid October, I was preparing to leave for a writing workshop in San Francisco. I still clung to my dream of writing and publishing fiction and even after full days of writing for the *Oregonian*, I tried to carve out time for my novel. While packing for the weeklong workshop, I learned a hunter was missing in Tillamook County.

Over the years, I've lost track of how many people have gone missing in the Coast Range. Most were just off on a leisurely hike. They fall off cliffs, into ravines, into rivers. They get lost and starve or fall prey to the wild. They get hurt and meet the same fate. And soon, the trees and brush, the weeds and moss claim the body, and their fate becomes one more unsolved Oregon mystery.

So it was with Jeromy Childress.

Despite all I needed to get done in one day's time for the trip to California, I knew I should do a story. I called the Tillamook sheriff's office and got directions to the site. I drove north for about fifty miles, then, turning at the tiny town of Beaver, twenty miles east on one of those backcountry roads where you see no one for long, long stretches of pavement. Eventually, I realized that somehow I'd missed my turn. Now I was lost. I turned and headed back the way I came, which is never a sure thing when you are lost in the vast and rugged country that is the Coast Range. I might add that I have no sense of direction and had no cell coverage and so I drove with a palpable sense of fear that now I, like the hunter, was quite possibly lost. Ten miles later, I found cell coverage and was able to get better directions. Finally, I made my way to the dirt road that five miles later led me to a small tent city. I'd been one of only a very few vehicles for miles and miles, but now I was surrounded by search and rescuers riding ATVs and horses, following dogs, carrying bullhorns, and studying maps. Overhead, a helicopter buzzed.

By now, Childress, thirty-one, had been missing for five days. I found his wife Kristen discussing search plans with a group of volunteers. She invited me into her camp and told me the story. She'd kissed her husband good-bye the Friday before as he left for his job as a bridge painter. He planned to go on his hunting trip directly from work with coworker Shane Luey and Luey's son, Shane Jr. She didn't expect to see him until sometime the next week. That Sunday, she left a message on his cell, not knowing that her husband had already been missing a full day.

Luey told police the trio had hunted all day Saturday. When they returned to their campsite, they realized they needed firewood, so they set out in the truck to find some. It was foggy; daylight turned to dusk, and soon they were lost. Nearly a full day later, they remained lost. The truck was low on gas, and they were again losing light. Childress was certain the campsite was just on the other side of a densely wooded hollow and suggested they set out on foot. But as they ventured deeper into the brush, Luey's son grew scared and father and son returned to the truck. That was the last anyone saw Jeromy Childress. A logger found the Lueys and guided them off the mountain.

Despite the fact that the odds of finding Jeromy in good health were growing increasingly low, Kristen, the energetic mom of a then three-year-old and seven-month old, was positive, even upbeat. She'd recruited dozens of friends to join the Tillamook County search teams, and she was convinced it was only a matter of time before they found him. It seemed she had good reason to hope. I'd heard reports of someone hearing three rapid gunshots—possibly a hunter's SOS and of someone finding a gum wrapper from the same kind Childress favored.

But deputies were less sure. Childress had been right about the campsite being just across the wooded hollow. What he probably didn't realize was that between him and the camp was Tucca Creek, a cold stream running four to five feet deep, bounded by sheer cliffs on both sides and cascading into waterfalls twelve to fifteen feet high. Cougars are common in the area, and the terrain is steep, uneven, and covered with brush.

Eventually, the search and rescue teams went home, and Childress's fate remained a mystery. The reports of the SOS and gum wrapper were apparently without merit; the deputies hadn't even known about them. A month later, I visited with Kristen at her home in Dayton for a follow-up story. Without Jeromy's paycheck, or whatever widow's benefits might be available because he hadn't been declared dead, she struggled to keep the family afloat. And she was still trying to figure out how to explain to her three-year-old that her Daddy wasn't coming home.

Kristen and I became friends, keeping in touch by phone. I sensed there was something she wasn't telling me, but I mostly dismissed the idea. Even if there was something, I wasn't going to push a newly widowed young mother for details she didn't want to share. She did admit she had her suspicions, and I did, too. Something wasn't right.

Still for months, even years, I expected Childress's body or at least his belongings to be revealed. And to this day, I never pass the turnoff in Beaver without wondering what really happened to Jeromy Childress?

Recently, I connected with his mother, Becky Grimes. My instincts that I did not know the full story had been true. Grimes told me her son was likely high at the time he went missing, high and possibly drunk or at least drinking, and that he'd had a scary run in with some drug dealers just weeks earlier in California.

"They went to Jeromy's hotel room, put a gun to his head, and forced him to drive them to the bank for money," Grimes said. "It scared my son to death. After that, they packed up their things and drove home. I would hate to think anyone from California came up and got him."

But she's puzzled, too, why her son would walk off into the dark with no flashlight, especially in the shape she suspected he must have been in.

"I'm sure they were drinking, and I know on the job there were a lot of nose drugs and Jeromy got pulled into that. He was up two to three days working and getting ready to go up there and hunt. He was in a daze. I pray every day that one day he'll be found, and we can bring him home. He was my only child. It's changed who I am, what I am. I don't even look the same anymore. I live a nightmare every single day."

TWO

DRIVING AND CRYING

2005

In the boat that February afternoon were three friends of nearly sixty years: Darhald Herrmann, sixty-eight; Norman Herrmann, seventy-five; and Herbert Littau, seventy. Just the guys and a boat and the Oregon coast. It doesn't get much better.

As boys they'd spent their days fishing and hunting together. They joined the military together, then came home and traveled together. When they settled down, they raised their families within a mile of each other. They'd started early that morning from their home in Shaw. The three of them shared a pickup cab, which pulled a trailered sixteen-foot skiff behind it. In Waldport, about one hundred miles southwest of their hometown, they unloaded the skiff into the bay and left the pickup in the port parking lot. At that early hour, the tide on Alsea Bay was high—a full to overflowing nine feet. But hours later, the tide turned, rushing out to ultimately reach a low of minus one—a ten-foot drop. The men found pulling the crab pots from the chilly waters of the bay impossible, so fast and furious was the water moving. Fishermen in another boat tried to help, but also failed. And so they decided it was time to call it a day and head in.

But, as they were about to learn, it was already too late.

First, the main engine failed, then the smaller back up engine also died, shorted by the rushing water. Their only hope was a paddle and a prayer. It would have almost been enough, if not for one simple mistake.

News of the capsizing reached me the next morning. I headed fifteen miles south to Waldport. Set on the Alsea Bay with a population of about two thousand, Waldport is popular for fishing, crabbing, kayaking, and enjoying the outdoors in general. It's a quiet community, made up of mostly working-class families, people who appreciate the contrasting beauty of the Coast Range forests and sandy bay front shores, where masses of seals sun themselves and bald eagles soar overhead.

I was in search of someone who might have witnessed the boating accident. One man at a seafood market on Highway 101 had seen the rescue crews race by, and feared the worst. When they returned a short time later, he was relieved, assuming it had been a false alarm. But aside from the market owner, I found no one to talk to. Town was deserted, likewise the parking lot at the boat loading ramp and a nearby restaurant. Finally, I gave up and headed for home to write. I called the desk to give them an update, which was basically that I had very little beyond a quote from the seafood market guy and the press release everyone else would use.

"Did you call the victims' wives?" my editor asked.

I had not. If approaching strangers and introducing myself was awkward, calling the family of someone who had just died was doubly so, and worse, it felt wrong. As much as I understood it was my job, and a crucial part of the story, I absolutely hated doing it. How could any newspaper story even begin to warrant such an intrusion at so difficult a time? And yet, I would learn, people often wanted to talk. They understood this was one of the last opportunities to tell the world why this person mattered. To share what had been lost. To proclaim their love and heartache and, maybe, let the world step just a bit closer to their lives. Of course, many times, they just wanted to tell you to go to hell, too.

On that day as I wound my way up 101, my editor heard my hesitation. It was all she needed.

"Sorry," she said, not sounding sorry at all. "You gotta make the call."

I dialed information as I drove, got phone numbers for two families, and called. Both lines went to voice mail. I left messages, both relieved to have avoided the intrusion, and disappointed because I knew that conversation, despite being difficult, would also make for a better story. I suspected another journalist might have tried harder, found another family member somewhere, somehow.

As I drove, I started figuring out how I'd write the story. I knew that the Coast Guard got a call just before 3:00 p.m. from Bill and Sandra Stevens, who had watched from their bay front home as the men struggled with the boat against the outpouring tide, then saw it cross the bay into the Pacific, turn broadside, and flip.

I knew that the water was about fifty-four degrees, survivable, depending on a number of factors—life vest, body composition, health, injuries— for as little as one hour or as many as six. I knew the search got underway at about 6:00 p.m. and that . . .

Wait. And finally, the little clapper gave a ding. If the call for help came in at 2:45 p.m., why the hell did they not start looking until six? I dialed the Coast Guard.

It turned out someone had made a mistake. A big one.

When the call came into the Coast Guard, the helicopter crew was in nearby Newport and immediately set off for Waldport, about a ten-minute flight, if that. Meanwhile, volunteers with the fire department drove over to the scene and saw a boat that matched the Stevens's description. But it wasn't in trouble. So they called the Coast Guard and told them no rescue was needed. And that was the end of the search.

But the Coast Guard always follows up on emergency calls, and that afternoon when they checked in with the Stevens, they learned that the boat the rescue crew had seen had had a canopy; the boat the Stevens watched capsize did not.

Three hours later, the search began anew. By 6:30 p.m., Darhald Herrmann was pulled from the water alive. Littau had died at sea. Norman Herrmann was still missing and presumed dead.

I was ready to write, but I still had no family comments. I tried once more. This time Norman Herrmann's wife, Rose, was at home and kind enough to take my call. She told me about the failing motor, the rushing tide. The last time anyone saw her husband he was hanging onto a couple buoys. She was hopeful he was still alive, but I could tell by her voice she knew that was so much wishful thinking.

I filed my story and considered it done. I should have known better. In the morning, my editor called. The survivor was taken to the local hospital, and it was up to me to go find him. If he was still there. And if I could get in to see him.

Hospitals generally expect reporters to contact the public relations person or whoever is in the position of authority to arrange for any interviews with patients or staff. The problem with that is by the time you've ground through the process, the patient has probably been discharged—and odds are, the hospital won't share any contact information. Obviously, the hospital is looking out for their patient. And obviously, your editor expects you to get around that.

I stashed my notebook in my purse, ambled up to the information desk and asked, just as polite and friendly as any hometown girl, for Herrmann's room number. It was that simple. I practically skipped down the hall.

I waltzed through a pair of doors, jumped on the elevator, and following the arrows toward the room numbers, found myself at a locked door with a sign: ICU unit. I tapped on the door. A nurse peeked out through a crack, "Can I help you?" I gave it every ounce of sweet talk I had, knowing as I blundered on, I was getting nowhere. The only way I had any chance of getting into Herrmann's room was through a family invitation. And they were all on the other side of the locked door. I asked the nurse to give them a message. She didn't say yes, but she didn't say no, either. Moments passed without any other sign of life. I started down the hall.

"Hello?"

I turned.

"Oh hi," I said, completely unprepared.

"I'm Evelyn, Darhald's wife. The nurse said you wanted to see me?"

"Uh, yes, I was hoping . . ."

She was friendly, but firm. He wasn't up to it. Maybe another time. Then, almost as an afterthought, she asked, "Do you know what happened?"

"I do," I said. "I wrote the story for the *Oregonian*."

"I mean what really happened? Why they weren't rescued sooner?"

"Yes," I said. "That's what I wrote. Do you have the paper?"

"No," she said. "I haven't seen it. I'll have to take a look."

"I have a copy," I said. "Let me go get it for you."

I raced down the hall and through the front doors, where the yellow box sat waiting. I dug through my purse for change and slipped the coins into the newspaper box, then hurried back, paper in hand, to the ICU.

Evelyn waited at the door. "Come on in," she said. "He'll talk to you."

Herrmann sat propped in his bed, a blue blanket tucked neatly around him, his blue eyes appraising me from beneath a head of closely cropped gray hair. Evelyn introduced me, but even before she'd gotten the words out, Herrmann was sweeping his strong arm through the air, beckoning me with a grin.

At sixty-eight-years-old, Herrmann was six years younger than my dad. Like my dad, he had served in the military, and like my dad, he was a working-class man. There was a comfort in Hermann and his wife, an instinctive knowledge that we came from the same place.

"Go ahead, sit down," Herrmann, a retired steelworker, said, patting the bed. I hesitated. "No really, it's okay," he said. I sat myself down at the edge of the bed, pulled out my notebook, pen, and tape recorder. I rarely used recorders because I don't trust them and because it takes too much time to transcribe the notes, but in situations where I wanted to get every last detail, I sometimes brought one along for back up.

Wednesday had started out like countless other days that saw the men sharing a boat on Alsea Bay. Then came the rushing tide, the failed engines, the doomed efforts to paddle against a force that was simply too great. Of the three, only Darhald Herrmann wore a flotation jacket. Norman Herrmann and Littau wore only life vests. Darhald managed to hang onto the overturned boat. Littau clung to some debris not far from him.

The minutes ticked by, then Darhald heard Littau call, "There it is," as he spotted the orange Coast Guard helicopter. It seemed already the old friends were saved. And then, just that quick, they watched in disbelief as it turned and flew away.

Littau, the oldest of the three and survivor of three bypass surgeries, was the first to give up the struggle and float away. Then Darhald's brother, Norman, was gone as well. Darhald Herrmann suspected he'd gotten tangled in the rope on the buoys and dragged down. The boat Hermann clung to was also sinking, and he knew he was about to be sucked down with it. He let go and began to swim.

"I swam and I swam and I swam," he said. "I never swam so much in my life."

He was one mile out to sea and one mile south of where the boat had flipped when a Good Samaritan skipper saw him floating in the water and pulled him into his boat. Herrmann recalled nothing of the rescue. His body temperature was eighty-one degrees, and he suffered cracked ribs, rope burns, and a very sore back. But even from his hospital bed, Herrmann was already planning the memorial he would build to his friends. "Maybe a monument on the hill for Norman and one for Herbert . . ."

And then he swallowed hard, his blue eyes filled with tears. I took his hand in mine and squeezed. Then, with the other, wiped dry my own cheeks.

A year passed, and I was beginning to gain some confidence. But just as I had heard before accepting the job, the demands were great and constant. While the majority of the people I worked with were truly good people, some were just rude, even unkind. Once, as I walked through the grocery store on a Saturday afternoon, a copy desk editor called to ask if I had checked to see if the casino opening I'd written about had actually taken place. I had not. It was the first time the subject had come up. As I stood there in the produce section, listening to her yell at me for not doing what she was sure my editor had instructed me to do (he had not), I remember wondering what the hell I had gotten myself into?

There were edits that came back at 10:00 p.m. with a thank you for getting to them quickly, after which the story was held for days. Once while I was on vacation, a photo editor called and asked me to contact a subject and reschedule. "I'm on vacation, and I don't have the story notes with me," I said, knowing he had all the information at his fingertips. "Look," he said, "Can you call anyway?" It was not a question.

But I developed my own coping skills. In time, I learned to shut down the computer at 6:00 p.m., or at the very least, leave work emails unopened. I ordered a second phone line with a distinct ring tone and refused to answer it in the evening unless I was sure I knew who was calling or was prepared to rush out into the night. Of course, if I didn't pick up the landline, odds were they'd call my cell.

The range of stories continued to broaden, and I was pleased to be writing not only news, but profiles and features—though the first-person pieces I favored remained off limits. I'd grown so accustomed to being summoned to hit the road, to never knowing for sure when I'd be home again, that I even kept a carry-on suitcase in my SUV packed with a change of clothing, toothbrush, makeup, and a night shirt. Just in case.

I was staying busy. I drove to Astoria for a premiere of *The Ring Two*, shot the summer before with a handful of locals cast as extras. The theater was packed, the mood festive as we awaited the show. Once it began, however, it didn't take long to realize the gleeful anticipation was for naught. Unbeknownst to the would-be local actors, nearly all of their scenes had been cut. I wrote about marine mammal strandings, a story that earned me a visit to the Hatfield Marine Science Center walk-in freezer filled with dead sea mammals. Soon, I would be headed back to Astoria to cover the trial of two women who stole their roommate's pain meds, abandoned her without food or water, then pushed the wheelchair with her dead body (bed sores infected to her bones) over a steep incline into a forty-foot-deep ravine.

There were not many dull moments, and that was a blessing. The reports coming from home about my dad's health were growing increasingly worse, and I knew it was a matter of months, maybe weeks, before he was gone. We bought tickets to fly to Pennsylvania and prayed we had enough time. But I had no idea the toll the daily calls with the constant barrage of bad news were taking until one day on the phone with my editor, I lost it and sobbed. However awkward it might have been, she was a comforting voice of calm and patience until I pulled myself together.

One week later, as I celebrated a 2-percent raise and a new contract, I got the phone call.

"It's time to come home, dear," my mother said by way of hello.

I grew up in a house three doors down from the house where my father was raised in central Pennsylvania—Amish country, home to Hershey chocolate and Lebanon bologna, land of shoo-fly pies and opera fudge, hoagies and hamboats, dippy eggs and scrapple.

Known to his friends as Toby, my dad was the storyteller in our family. Whether on the front porch, at the local tavern, or around the kitchen table, he would tell some tale from his day, usually one ending with a laugh, occasionally something he'd witnessed that had left him scratching his head.

When I first brought my husband home, my dad wasted no time in sharing the stories he'd cataloged from my childhood. Like the time my parents took me for my first bra at J. C. Penney's. It was determined I would need a size 28AAA. As we were leaving, my dad reported I'd told the clerk, "I'll need a bigger one when we come back." How he laughed at that. Or the year they'd already bought me two winter coats, but I'd found another I was in love with. He still had the note I wrote to plead for a third, which read in my eleven-year-old scrawl, "If you buy me the coat, I won't ask for another until next year."

My dad was also likely responsible for my newspaper habit. Besides auto racing magazines, he wasn't much of a reader, but every night, his ritual after work included a quart of beer and the local *Lebanon Daily News*. Likewise, we always had the Sunday paper, the *Harrisburg Patriot*, owned by the same company that owns the *Oregonian*.

I just happened to be home visiting eight years earlier when my dad, then a vibrant sixty-seven-year-old, announced I'd better take him to the hospital. He was having chest pains and though so far as we knew there was nothing wrong with his heart, heart disease had taken his father and two of his brothers, as well as one nephew, who died at forty-three.

The news from the doctors was good. It wasn't his heart, but a stomach aneurysm. My grandmother had had the same thing. The doctors told him to go home, quit smoking, and they'd schedule surgery. The next day, after five decades of filterless Lucky Strikes and Pall Malls, he quit. Never smoked another cigarette again. But today I would tell him, Dad, smoke the cigarettes, take your chances with the aneurysm. But whatever you do, stay the hell away from the doctors.

The surgeon repaired the aneurysm, then decided to do some work on an artery in his leg that was somehow related to an old Korean War wound. First came the staph infection, then the technicians collapsed a lung, and once, they forgot him in the basement where he'd been taken for x-rays. By the time someone found him, my father, a man with two Purple Hearts, was so damned cold and despairing, he was in tears.

Finally, they sent him home. But his health never really improved. Rather, he began dying slowly, declining day by day, year after year. In the end, he couldn't breathe, couldn't walk, couldn't even properly piss. He signed a do-not-resuscitate (DNR) order and made my mother promise there would be no nursing homes. I was old enough to remember his father in a nursing home: the diapers, the bedpans, the haunted stare. It was not the ending I wanted for my dad.

I couldn't begin to count how many stays he logged at the veteran's hospital, a mammoth old-stone building set amid sprawling lawns where doctors in brightly colored golf clothes practiced their swings. It was always something: pneumonia, prostate troubles, a mild stroke. This time, it was a blockage in his stomach. There was nothing to do but take him into surgery, and the only way they could do that was to put him on a ventilator and hope, once the surgery was done, that they could get him off of it without killing him. But that's not the way it happened. Pneumonia flared. Again. Finally, the doctors agreed to take him off the ventilator.

And so, in April 2005, nearly a decade after that first trip to the ER, I boarded the plane expecting to see my dad alive for the last time, and to witness death in person for the second. The first happened thirty-seven years earlier as I sat at a racetrack squeezed between my mom and dad. We were there to watch Dad's old racing buddy, Bert Brooks, a premier race car driver. When the race was over, Bert was coming over for a barbecue and I, one of the few girls in the neighborhood, wasted no time boasting about that fact.

We arrived at the race in Hershey early that day so Dad could go see Bert in the pits, but we hadn't arrived early enough and the pits were already closed. The Hershey stadium was packed with twenty thousand spectators; the sky was a sort of uninspired gray, but not really threatening rain. The drivers lined up, the flag went down, and off they went around the oval track. I don't know how many laps they were into the race before the yellow caution flag came out. Brooks slowed to allow another driver to enter the pit, but the drivers behind him must not have seen the flag. Two cars slammed into Brooks. His open cockpit car stood on end, balanced for a moment, then fell, crushing—as my eight-year-old mind processed it—Bert Brooks's head beneath it. As one the crowd gasped, and as one, fell silent.

"Oh, Toby," my mom said.

"I know," my dad said, standing, hands on hips, staring across that gray divide. We watched in near silence as the ambulance carried Brooks away, then the drivers took their place on the track and the race resumed. It wasn't long after that the loud speakers crackled. At forty-eight, Bert Brooks was dead. They halted the race. We had a moment of silence, and we all went home.

This time, nearly four decades later, I knew I was going to watch the loss of another life, and I had no idea if I was up for it, but I was determined to be strong, determined to be there for my father for whatever he needed.

My niece met us at the airport with the news that the doctors had changed their minds. They wanted to try a new antibiotic—a new antibiotic so they could cure him of pneumonia and send him to a nursing home where he would continue to waste away depressed and diapered, attached to all manner of machines doing the work his body no longer could.

We walked into the hospital room and found my formerly handsome, lean, and muscled dad bloated with water, his full head of once thick dark hair finally gray, his skin ashen, and a look in his eyes of such utter despair it nearly brought me to my knees. There were tubes up his nose, in his mouth, in his arms, and in his penis. His hands were strapped to the bed so he couldn't pull them out, an attempt he made any chance he got, the nurses said. He wanted to die. I wanted him to die, but I could not summon the courage to disconnect him from the support keeping him alive. We told him we loved him, and we wanted to do anything we could to make him comfortable. He squeezed my hand and winked at me. I removed the restraints. He gestured to Chan to free him from the machines. We just stood there feeling utterly helpless and cowardly. But I thought about it. I thought about it every damned minute. I imagined the scenarios. My dad gasping for air, in pain. The alarms. The panic. What if it took forever and he suffered the whole time? And there was the other more selfish consideration: would I go to prison?

For two days, we asked the nurse, "When are you going to take him off the machines?" He did, after all, have a signed DNR. Unfortunately, he'd agreed to the ventilator for the surgery, and apparently that changed everything.

"We're waiting for George," the nurses said.

There was no sign of when it would end, so Chan returned to Oregon to take care of the dogs and go back to work. I had no sick leave and no vacation time, and wasn't sure how I was going to manage without pay for a couple of weeks, but when it came up in a phone call with my editor, she immediately reassured me they had my back. She was good to her word. I didn't lose an hour of pay.

I passed the days sitting by my dad's bed, watching TV with him. I wet little sponges on the end of lollypop sticks and swabbed his mouth. I bought a small stereo and his favorite Johnny Cash CDs. I bought him the scratch-off lottery tickets for which he was famously lucky. But he was no longer interested in trying his luck. He knew. We all knew. His luck had run out.

On day three, the mystery man George finally appeared. George, it turned out, was a surgeon. He was a big, oafish man with trailing shoelaces. He gathered us in the small room reserved for such purposes. "You're denying my father a good death," I said. He said they would give my dad three more days to see if he could breathe on his own. If not, they would take him off the life support Friday. If that happened, and we all believed it would, they would take him off the ventilator, then give him oxygen and morphine. With the buildup of carbon dioxide and depletion of oxygen in his blood, he wouldn't be aware of much for long.

As we filed from the room, I turned to George, "If you don't tie your shoe, you're going to trip and break your neck."

He looked at me like an errant sixth-grader just scolded at recess.

This was the man in charge of my father's life and death?

Friday morning, I drove to the VA. It was a perfectly sunny spring day. The rest of the family was already there, and we went into my father's room as a group. I took one of Dad's hands. Mom took the other. I tried to be strong, stoic. I tried to be all those things I never am, and failed. The tears rolled down my cheeks. My mom turned to me with that look I knew better than to ignore. "Stop it now," she said in her low, no bullshit tone. "You will not upset him." I turned away from the hospital bed and wiped my cheeks with my free hand. The doctor came in and removed the breathing tube and restraints. They slipped on an oxygen mask. My dad opened his eyes, and finally, smiled. "There's Lori and Tabby and Beulah Ann," he said naming me, my niece, and his sister. He looked happy. He looked as though he had just awoken from a holiday dinner nap, and at any moment might request a slice of my mom's pie. He looked like he might swing his legs from the bed and announce he was going for a quick beer. He looked like my dad. Toby. I squeezed his hand. His eyelids drooped. They started the morphine drip. We watched the monitor as his heartbeat slowed, the blue line on the screen nearly flat. The nurse disconnected the monitor and pushed it away from his bed. Not long after he was gone.

I cut the ID bracelet from his wrist and walked outside to cry alone.

And so began the days of driving and crying as I traveled up and down the coast following the next story. There was something about being alone in the car, driving for hours, logging miles on an often-empty highway that lent itself to a good cry. No telling what passers-by must have thought or how often I showed up at the hotel, the interview, the restaurant, oblivious to my red-eyes and puffy face.

Less than a month after burying my father, I wrote about a young woman burying her mother. Strawberry Hill is a state wayside five miles south of Yachats where low-lying areas carpeted in thick brush give way to higher forested knolls and even higher cliffs with endless views of the coastline. On the Saturday before Mother's Day, Tevina Benedict, fifty-four, traveled with her daughter Erica Benedict-Barta's college class to study tidal pools and shell middens. She took a walk deep into the densely brushed headlands to relieve herself and never returned. On Mother's Day, they found her at the bottom of a seventy-foot cliff, skull, neck, back, ribs, and sternum broken. Likely as not, she took one step too many, one step that fell not on solid dense brush, but overhanging salal and grass. To say it happens all the time would be an overstatement, but it is not rare. In the two weeks after Benedict's death, two others had to be rescued from cliffs north in Tillamook County. Two years prior, the executive producer of the reality show *Cops* fell to his death there as well.

That summer, stories began surfacing in the national news about the safety of our nation's highways. My editors and I decided I would drive Highway 101, border to border, for a story on the condition of the highway—a winding, mostly two-lane, stretch of asphalt peppered with pullouts opening to oceanfront vistas that draw travelers from all over the world. Chan and I left on a Thursday in July, driving up to Astoria to spend the night, then rising early to drive across the Megler-Astoria Bridge and back just so we could say we started at milepost zero. It took the better part of the day to make Brookings, a 363-mile trip. Along the way, we counted log trucks and bicycles while lamenting the danger of the combination of the two. Once, we found ourselves facing an oversized load that had veered into our lane so as not to take out the cyclists on the shoulder. There was enough space between us, so it was not so much a close call as a reminder of how quickly and easily a mundane drive can morph into the potential kiss of death. But that aside, the drive was fairly uneventful, and I worried what would I do for a story. There had been no great traffic jams, no accidents, we hadn't even got hung up behind the usual parade of sluggish RVs. What was the story?

In the morning, I awoke to news of a fatal accident that took the life of a sheriff's deputy when a sixteen-year-old tried to pass a car on Highway 101 in Tillamook County and hit the deputy's motorcycle head on. Next, I opened an email and read of a three-car fatal accident just a few miles from where the deputy died. Two days later, I learned of a third fatality, roughly fifteen miles from the others. The last occurred when a truck failed to make a steep curve and plowed through a building. A week after the border-to-border trip, I headed north for the deputy's funeral. Coming through the curves of Cloverdale I saw what had been The Shell Game, a shop that had carried seashells from all over the world, now a wrecked heap of wood and glass and debris. I pulled over and approached a woman surveying the damage. As I grew closer, I introduced myself, prompting a response of anger and tears. It seemed I had somehow caused her grief anew, and I had no idea why, or how to comfort her. Puzzled, I crossed the highway and went back to my car. It made no sense. I could understand her not wanting to talk with me, but the ranting and tears. I needed to know. What had I done? I crossed the highway again to the pile of rubble where she stood still.

"I'm sorry to intrude," I said. "But are you upset with me for some reason?"

Still crying, she apologized. It wasn't me. It was everyone. Lois Peterson had operated The Shell Game since 1987. Her two cats were inside when the truck crashed through the building. One suffered a broken leg, and it had taken days to find the other cat, huddled frightened in the ruin. Her whole life had been that shop. People had stopped there year after year, seeking the shells Peterson shipped in from exotic places all over the globe. And now it was gone.

Lois took some time to heal and then built a new Shell Game. Often, as I drove home from covering some story on the north coast, I'd stop and visit, stretch my legs and check out the shells that filled display cases. In that same way, I began to make friends up and down the coast, people who I had met through tragic circumstances, who welcomed me into their lives long after.

That summer, the *Oregonian* office manager called to say correspondents could no longer use business cards with the *Oregonian* printed on them, and I would need to mail whatever cards I had left back to her. I persuaded her that I would burn them. But it left me with a bad feeling. People often asked for a business card, the only real evidence I had of being affiliated with the paper. Without a business card, all I had was my word. While it had nothing to do with my efforts, and everything to do with the state's regulations about contract employees, it still left me feeling somehow second rate. My sense of job security, whatever that may have been, was also fading.

By then, we were down from six correspondents to just three. One had left in a dispute with an editor, another had been let go for financial reasons—or so I was told. And a third had quit. My editor tried to reassure me, but never neglected to add that there were no guarantees.

It seemed my only hope of security was to keep landing front page stories, to keep running hard and fast and hopefully prove myself worth the expense. That's where my head was on a day in late September when I answered the phone and found my husband on the other end.

"Hey, do you know that three people died crossing the Umpqua River bar last night?" Chan asked.

"What are you talking about?" I said. "Where did you hear that?"

"Everyone's talking about it," he said. By everyone, he meant his fellow linemen and their many contacts, most of whom had spent a good part of their lives, if not all, in Lincoln County. If there was news or gossip or rumors, there was a very good chance they would hear it first.

Instantly, there was the buzz of dread that came with the knowledge I'd missed something. I called my editor. She found the press release. No, she said. There were no fatalities. It says two people were rescued.

I repeated what Chan had told me. My editor began reading the press release out loud. She was nearly to the end of several paragraphs, and there, in one of the last sentences, she found it. Two bodies found, one missing—presumed dead.

"Shit." It was already coming up on 1:30. Winchester Bay was a good hour and a half drive if I pushed it.

"We'll have to do it by phone," she said.

"No," I said, envisioning the competition's A1 headline; my bottom of the fold, page B2 tale. Three people had died, once again on an outing that should have been fun, that should have ended with fish tales and souvenir photographs. Instead, something had gone wrong. What? If I left right away, I could be there at 3, 3:30 latest. What did we have to lose?

"But . . ." she said.

"I can make it, and I can file from there."

"Go!"

Winchester Bay has a population of less than five hundred. It is home to the Umpqua River Lighthouse and hugely popular with ATVers, as well as fishermen, crabbers, and beachcombers.

The only story I'd done there previously was on plans to restrict ATV use in the dunes. If you ever feel the need to piss people off en masse, just talk about taking away their ATV terrain.

I didn't have any close contacts in Winchester Bay; I wasn't even sure of the lay of the land. But it is small, so I figured it couldn't be too hard to find what I needed. When I finally arrived, town was quiet and mostly empty. Nothing suggested the terrible tragedy that had occurred the night before. I drove into the harbor, parked, and walked into a café. It was empty and about to close. I asked the young woman if she knew anything. She said she didn't want to talk about it, the media had been bugging her all day. Go talk to Sully, she said. He saw the whole thing.

Really? Someone saw it? Where do I find him?

Actually, that's him right there, she said, pointing to a pickup truck with a boat hitched behind it.

Just as the people in Garibaldi take to the jetties to watch the boats cross the bar, people in Winchester Bay have their own vantage point from the Umpqua River Lighthouse property on the hill above. Patrick "Sully" Sullivan had watched as the weather worsened throughout the day, and warned other boaters to get back in by 2:00 p.m. when the tide would turn. That evening he was worried about his friend Richard Oba, who captained the Sydney Mae II. Standing there on the hill, he saw the Sydney Mae II's light, then heard the boom he recognized as the sound of fiberglass hitting rock. He called the Coast Guard, and the search and rescue was on. Only Oba and passenger James Parker survived. Dead were Ginger Strelow, the sixty-four-year-old office manager for Oba's Pacific Pioneer Charters, and charter boat clients Bill Harris, sixty-six, of Springfield and Paul Turner, seventy-six, of Idaho.

I asked Sully what he thought happened. The bar was closed, he said. Oba should have never been there.

Four words—the bar was closed—and it was a whole different story.

At the nearby Coast Guard station, the chief confirmed Sully's story. Coast Guard crewmembers talked by phone with Oba several times. The last time was at about 8:00 p.m. in a conversation with the Coast Guard communications watchstander. "I told him that the bar was still restricted to all recreational vessels and uninspected vessels," he told me. "The captain replied, 'Fine. I'll take my passengers to Coos Bay, but it will be even more dangerous.' That was when the phone cut out; he was angry, and I thought he had hung up on me."

I sat down at a picnic table in the park and wrote the story on my laptop. The owners of the café were still hanging around and were kind enough to let me file the story from a back booth. Wi-Fi was alive and well, but on the Oregon coast you still needed a phone line to connect. I hung around for edits since I'd have no cell coverage for much of the drive home, then finally hit the road. I was exhausted, but I knew I'd made the right call in driving there for the story. I cracked the windows, cranked the stereo, and sang—tactics I often used when I was beat and needed to stay alert.

That night, I got a call from the only surviving passenger, Jim Parker, who wanted his story told. It was late, but I couldn't run the risk of waiting until morning. What if Parker changed his mind or I wasn't able to reach him? So I pulled on the headset, and let my fingers fly across the keyboard as he recounted for me minute by minute the accident that almost took his life.

All day he'd listened to the boat radio warning skippers not to attempt to cross the Umpqua River bar. But as they drew closer to the bar, Oba seemed to think the ocean had quieted down, and he could make it safely across, Parker said.

"He said, 'I could probably make it,'" Parker recalled. "I said, 'The

Coast Guard says it's closed.' We're getting closer, I stand up. We are two hundred yards, maybe one hundred yards out, and I turn around, and I see this wave above me. With the deck lights, it was really illuminated. It looked like a big yellow wall. It would have taken anyone."

Three months later, I was settling in to enjoy Christmas Eve when I got word that the National Transportation Safety Board (NTSB) had come out with its finding on the capsizing. Skipper Richard Oba was at fault. I'd tried to reach Oba several times for earlier stories, but he'd never take my call. Still, that afternoon, I dialed his number once again just to say I'd tried. To my surprise, he was willing to talk. But he didn't say much. The report contained inconsistencies, he said. "In time, the true story will come out."

A year and a half later, in the spring of 2007, Oba became the first captain on the West Coast to be convicted of a 154-year-old maritime statute known as Seaman's Manslaughter. The US Attorney's office asked for a sentence of about three-and-a-half years. US District Judge Ancer Haggerty shocked the courtroom when he instead sentenced Oba to six years in federal prison for the "reckless" accident.

And that was the end of my reporting on Richard Oba. Likewise, it seems, the rest of the media. But as it turned out, the case didn't end there. Years later, I learned that Oba had appealed the sentence. In a decision filed in March 2009, the US Court of Appeals agreed that Oba had acted "recklessly," but also found that Judge Haggerty had given insufficient justification for imposing a sentence "roughly 40 percent higher" than sentencing guidelines called for. The Appeals Court also noted "that the captain of the Staten Island ferry whose illegal drug use at the helm led to 11 deaths received a below-Guidelines sentence of 18 months imprisonment after pleading guilty to 11 counts of Seaman's Manslaughter." By the time the court made the decision, Oba had been in custody at the Federal Prison Camp in Atwater, California, since August 2007. He was released in 2011.

In the fall of 2005, talk on the northern Oregon coast and well beyond centered on the Lewis and Clark Bicentennial. The five-day signature event, "Destination: The Pacific," was one of fourteen sanctioned by the National Council of the Lewis and Clark Bicentennial and would be held in November at various sites throughout Clatsop County. It was one of the rare stories I got to cover that wasn't all doom and gloom, and involved an October hike on the Fort to Sea Trail, built as part of the bicentennial celebration. The six-and-a-half-mile trail starts at Fort Clatsop and ends at the beach on a wood platform overlooking the sea. It is meant to give hikers an idea of the journey the original Lewis and Clark expedition might have taken themselves in traveling from their shelter to the Pacific.

On a Saturday, Chan and I set out with the park ranger from the visitor center at the Lewis and Clark National Historical Park. Only weeks before, the Fort Clatsop replica, built in 1955, had been destroyed by fire, and the scent of burned wood still sweetened the air. Leaving the Fort Clatsop Visitor Center, we climbed to the top of Clatsop Ridge then down through the dense, dark woods, alert to the possibility of seeing all manner of wildlife, including elk, bear, bald eagles, and cougars. I mentioned earlier that I am morbidly afraid of two things. There's the problem with heights, of course. And then, there's snakes. Thank God I didn't know at the start of the hike that I was about to be offered a twofer.

I wasn't always frightened of snakes. We'd had them as pets in elementary school, and while I stood in the hall and cried at feeding time, I was not afraid of them. Then came a day in Denver when I walked into my second-floor office and found several small figurines on the floor. Huh, I thought, the cats don't usually jump up here. I bent to pick them up and place them back on the top of a small bookshelf, and that's when I saw it. My first thought was, I don't have a toy snake, which in a microsecond morphed into ohmygodthatsnotatoy. I cleared a half dozen steps in one leap, grabbed the phone, and called my husband.

"How big is it," he asked.

"How big is it? Who the hell cares how big it is . . ."

It was, in fact, only about a foot long. A poor little garter snake that somehow had found its way to the top of a bookshelf on the second floor of my house. How it got there remains a mystery. The cat might have brought it in, or it may have hitched a ride in a duffel bag I'd recently brought in from the garage, or as a fish and wildlife ranger suggested, slipped into my husband's wetsuit, which happened to be hanging in the closet next to the bookshelf and which he had recently worn for a white-water trip. (He absolutely refuses to believe this is a possibility.) I ran for my neighbor, Ron, who was raised in Kansas and was an old hand at dealing with rattlesnakes. Ron marched up the stairs, then returned seconds later, holding the snake by the tail.

"This it?" he asked.

I've been terrified ever since.

So there I was, maybe thirty minutes into our lovely recreational hike, when my dear husband says, "Don't freak out, Lori, but a snake just nearly ran over your boot. I can't believe you didn't see it." Now the way I look at it, since I didn't see it, why tell me? But guys look at things differently. He figured he was doing me a favor by warning me to watch out. From then on, I might as well have been on a death march. I tried to keep my eyes averted from the ground, but knew if there was a snake slithering within a mile, I'd spot it. Finally, after what seemed like forever, we cleared the dark, damp woods and came onto a section of the trail that is an open meadow, soon giving way to sandy dunes and the roar of the surf beckoning. I relaxed. This was my kind of hiking. Any moment now, we would reach the beach. Then we came to the bridge. And as it turned out, the bridge—roughly twenty feet above Neacoxie Lake—was not finished. Our guide decided that what we needed to do was walk single file across a board, only inches wide, while hanging on to a piece of rope (which looked more like string to me). I tried. I wanted to be a trooper, I did. I so wanted not to be the chicken-shit city girl who was afraid of everything. Our guide suggested I could walk behind Chan, eyes closed, while clinging to his belt. I thought that might work. I grasped Chan's leather belt and closed my eyes. And that's where that little experiment ended. Not even one step. It wasn't that I wouldn't. It was that I couldn't. It was that simple. Looking back, I see it was idiotic to even suggest it. What if I had taken that blind trek, and fallen into the water below?

Instead, we took a detour through the brush until we could connect with the trail on the other side of the lake. It seemed like a fine alternative to me. What was an extra twenty minutes? It wasn't the kind of place you expect to see snakes, and we would be at ground level. We sure would be—at ground level, where orb weaver spiders sat fat in the middle of webs strung from bush to bush. The park ranger, already mildly miffed at the delay, grimly lifted strand after strand of fine silk, gingerly disconnecting the tenuous tie across our path, allowing us to pass. He was none too happy with me; I thought it served him right.

But finally, we reached the beach.

THREE

DEADLY ELEMENTS

2006

We started our New Year at sea on a catamaran off Puerto Vallarta. With the exception of some early seasickness on my part, it was the perfect day—calm blue seas, clear skies, and all manner of sea life, most memorably the manta rays that launched themselves from the sea, catching air for several feet before crashing with a bang back into the water. Chan had taken a spot with several others up front on the netted trampoline between the hulls. It seemed safe enough or at least no one warned him away. We set sail early in the morning, then anchored at a spot where guests could try their hand at snuba diving, a hybrid of snorkeling and scuba diving in which the diver is tethered to a raft carrying the compressed air. Others took quick lessons in scuba diving. We had lunch on board, then stopped offshore from an island. Some people swam in; others caught a ride on a small boat. Once on land we shopped with the locals and ordered drinks from open air bars. All in all, it was an idyllic day.

Late afternoon, we headed back to port, stopping along the way to drop off passengers from other marinas. All day, the netting had provided a comfortable front-row seat for Chan and others to see the action. But now as we crossed back out to sea, the water suddenly grew rough, bouncing the catamaran, slapping it hard against the surf. And there was Chan, hanging on with all he had as the chop threw him from the netting into the air. The crew said nothing, but eyed him with concern. It was too late to do anything; moving from the net while the boat was in motion would have been even more treacherous. His only choice was to hang on and try to ride it out.

Of course, no one wore life jackets, and that was an irony I was not finding amusing at the moment.

On that very same day in Oregon, New Year's Day, my story about legislative efforts to make life jackets mandatory on charter boats was the A1 centerpiece. The move was led by a friend of Bill Harris, who died in the *Sydney Mae II* capsizing, and opposed by just about everyone in the industry. Even the Coast Guard said it would be too burdensome to manage.

Local skipper Jim Edson, who operated Yaquina Bay Charters told me, "It's not their call to make. I've been doing this a long time. We don't go if it's really rough. The one thing they don't tell you is these life jackets are horrible. They're terrible to be in."

Now, as I watched Chan—by then, the sole person on the trampoline—lift and drop, lift and drop, I couldn't help think about the headline if something tragic were to happen. He shouldn't have been up there. It was that simple. But we were on vacation; we weren't thinking of danger. We were having fun. And besides, if it was a risky place to ride, the crew would have said so. Right?

In time, the surf calmed, and Chan made his way to a seat by me for the last leg back to port. He was safe, but we would keep that memory with us, a reminder—one I of all people shouldn't have needed—that in the tick of a clock circumstances can turn ugly even in the best of times.

The legislation mandating life jackets on Oregon charter boats never really went anywhere. Boat captains said it would take too much time and effort to get life jackets on everyone and that it would cause extensive wear and tear on the jackets. And so, that was the end of that, but it wouldn't be the last I wrote about life jackets and Jim Edson.

Back home from Mexico, I visited a doctor in Lincoln City for the longest, most drawn out employment physical ever. Such was the price of admission to the rank of staff writer at the *Oregonian*. I would still be paid for only thirty hours a week—the same as before—but I would have vacation time, medical benefits, a 401k, and be included in newsroom training.

But first, the physical. Of course, everyone knew the only real reason for the physical was to see if I was smoking pot or snorting something or abusing any prescription drugs. I was not, and on a day in January I made the trip to Portland to receive my various prizes: my security badge; a supply of reporter's notebooks; and a file that must have been six inches thick on health care, retirement, and rules I was to live by entitled "How to Stay out of Trouble at *The Oregonian*."

I was excited that I would finally be a full-fledged member—albeit part time—of the *Oregonian*, but I was also sorry to be losing my freedom (however little I actually had) and still harbored the fantasy of someday spending my days writing fiction and creative nonfiction instead of always chasing down the latest news.

Days later, during a conversation with my editor, I learned I would have to resign from my position on the Newport Library Board of Directors and Library Foundation. The reasoning was that it was a city-owned entity and if anything criminal or otherwise occurred, I would not be able to cover it. I had been chair of the first Newport Reads, had spent months helping choose the first book and planning the community celebration. Now, days before the event was to launch, one day before I was scheduled to appear on a radio show as a guest representing Newport Reads, I had no choice but to resign.

My personal involvement in the community at large pretty much ended there.

On February 7, the phone woke me just after 6:00 a.m., and I instinctively went from groggy to wide awake—or at least feigning a reasonable semblance thereof—in a matter of seconds. There was a time when an early phone call awoke me with dread, signaling the possibility of bad news from home. But I knew by then it was likely some word of breaking news. That morning, I found Tillamook County Sheriff Todd Anderson on the other end of the line. I had worked with Anderson on a couple of stories—most notably the Morris family murders—and I was just getting to know him.

He was calling to tell me that a commercial fishing vessel, the Catherine M, had gone down at about 1:30 a.m. on or near the Tillamook Bay bar, the same bar where the *Taki-Tooo* was lost. Two men, crewman Trona Griffin, thirty, and skipper Craig Larsen, thirty-two, were missing; only the body of deceased crewman Jeff King, thirty, had been found. Debris from the forty-one-foot boat littered two miles of the beach. I fed the stories to my editors by phone. We were finally getting serious about posting web stories and keeping our web content up to date. At first, I hated the posts. I thought it ruined the freshness of the story for the morning paper. But I eventually came to see the posts as one more way to reach an audience and came to enjoy the immediacy of them. As naive as it seems now, I never expected the web to actually replace the paper. Nor did I foresee that it would ultimately cost me my job.

In Garibaldi, I stopped at a port restaurant, sipping diet soda at the counter, hoping for someone who knew anything to wander in, but the place was deserted. Back at the jetty, I approached a man in a pickup truck. As it turned out, he was the commercial fisherman who saw the boat's distress flares, saw the vessel lights go dark, and called the Coast Guard. And then he told me another story.

Nineteen years, eleven months, and thirty days prior—February 8, 1986—the fifty-two-foot F/V *Miss Dana* capsized while going out over the Tillamook bar. Three men died in the capsizing, including Jeff King's twenty-one-year-old uncle, George Vandecoevering.

I drove home exhausted. I'd been at it since taking Anderson's call that morning. I'd logged at least four hours on the road, fed posts all day, and still needed to write the newspaper version and file it. By the time I dealt with edits it would be well into the evening. I was looking forward to a good night's sleep and an easy, low-key day. But before I even made it home, I had a call from my editor with the next day's assignment. Suspected cold-case killer James Braman Jr. had been arrested in Toledo for the November 3, 1975, double homicide of Frank Hinkley, forty-five, and girlfriend, Barbara Rosenfield, forty-two, at a strip club in south Seattle. The pair had been shot at close range with a .45 caliber pistol.

After going unsolved for decades, the King County sheriff's office had reopened the case and come up with new evidence and two witnesses. One witness was a student at the University of Washington. Not long before the killings, Braman had borrowed the student's pickup and a .45-caliber semiautomatic pistol, saying he had been in a fight and needed protection. Later, he met the student at the library. As they walked, Braman threw his jacket away and his shoes into a lake. Another witness told deputies Braman confessed to killing Hinkley, who was like a father to him, because

Hinkley had caught him with his hands in the till. He shot Rosenfield because she was a witness.

Braman also told the witness that as Rosenfield was on her knees, he said, "You wouldn't believe what a .45-caliber slug does to someone's head."

Braman, fifty-six, had been diagnosed with liver cancer and had less than six months to live. My editors wanted me to get an early start looking for people who knew him. By noon the next day, I'd figured out where Braman had hung out and set out to belly up to the bar of several watering holes, joking with my editor that if this bar hopping continued, I'd be wearing Depends.

In downtown Newport, I sat by a man playing lottery slots. He wasn't particularly keen on talking to me, but after he had a string of wins, I suggested I must be good luck, and he began to warm up. He told me of the time Braman had spit on a man during a poker game, then Maced him. "But you didn't hear that from he," he said.

Later, at the Siletz Roadhouse, locals gathered around the pub weighed in with comments: Braman was physically inept, a heavy smoker with a limp and a bad back, certainly not someone you'd expect to have the guts to murder someone. Others said he was an irritable know-it-all who fancied himself a better poker player than he actually was. Still, others described a typical dad who worried about his sons and kept a low profile around town.

I called my editor. Spitting on someone didn't a murderer make, but it did speak to his character. But no, she said, I couldn't use that in a story unless I talked to the man who had actually been spit on. I knew the man's name. I knew he was a cab driver. I also knew I was tired and wanted the story done. At a parking lot between downtown and Newport's Bayfront, I pulled up to a trio of Yellow Cabs, and asked if any happened to be the cabby I was seeking. They were not, but they told me where to find him.

I knocked on the door of a little rental cottage in Nye Beach, then stood back so whoever might look out the window would have a clear view of me. He was wary of me before I even managed those six little words: "I'm Lori Tobias with the *Oregonian*," and it occurred to me that in the rankings of who people are least pleased to see at their door, reporters came in only behind the police and IRS.

The cab driver didn't want to talk about Braman, and he especially did not want his name used. He simply didn't trust the guy.

"But he's dying," I said.

He shook his head. He didn't even trust that. In the end, he confirmed that Braman had spit on him, had, in fact, done such things to others routinely. But I was not to dare use his name.

I filed one story, then continued following the wranglings between the DA, the public defender, the Seattle judge, and local judge, while Braman watched from a camera in his cell. He looked weak and in pain. First, the judge called for $50,000 bail and then Braman could go home to die, but scant hours later, a second judge reversed that decision and set bail at $5 million—an impossible amount that would keep Braman locked up. Minutes after filing that story, I learned that he was, in fact, free on bail.

Two weeks after his arrest, he died of an overdose of methadone prescribed for his pain. Braman went to his grave refusing to talk about the crimes, telling police, "They'll kill me," and also that he had three sons and "killing one of them would mean nothing to them."

Days later came word that a young man was missing, his car found parked along the side of Highway 101 on the south end of Willapa Bay in Washington. The only sign of the car's twenty-nine-year-old owner, John Puglisi, were a few pieces of clothing, including his pants with his car keys in the pocket, and footprints in the mud. From the looks of it, the Yale grad friends called J. P. had set out to walk to a land mass called Baby Island. That was Friday. There was no other sign of Puglisi, only a report to police of a naked or nearly naked man with a backpack on the banks of the bay. At the time, the wind was blowing about thirty knots, or thirty-five miles per hour, and there were whitecaps on the water.

It didn't take long before the talk turned to mud, the kind that can trap and kill you. One biologist at the nearby Willapa National Wildlife Refuge described it as having the consistency of black mayonnaise. I knew that mud.

In Alaska, when people talk about the danger of the mud flats, the story of Adeana Dickison is likely to come up. Dickison was an eighteen-year-old newlywed who became stuck in the mud near Girdwood in July 1988. She and her husband had recently relocated to Alaska from Nevada and were driving an all-terrain four-wheeler on the mud flats when it became stuck. Dickison tried to push from behind, but her leg became trapped in the mud. For hours her husband and would-be rescuers worked to free her as the tide rushed in. When the water rose over her head, they gave her a tube to breathe through and kept working to free her. In the end, the mud and tide won.

For me that story has always had a particularly chilling effect. I was eighteen, new to Anchorage, where I had traveled to help my sister with her toddler son so she could go on maneuvers with the Air Force. I was feeling a certain young woman's glee that spring had finally arrived, grabbed my brother-in-law's bicycle, and took off. I had no idea of how to get around the city and knew it would take only a couple turns and I'd be lost. So once I hit the main road, I decided I would ride straight only and make no turns. It had been months, maybe a year, since I'd been on a bike, and the freedom, the relaxation, the possibility of adventure that always came with being atop two wheels was a song in my heart. And so I rode for miles and miles until I came to the end of earth and found myself on the edge of Knik Arm. Fancy that, I'd ridden to the beach. I dropped the bike in the grass and crept down a slight incline, then stepped onto what I assumed would be sand. Instead, my foot found only mud and instantly it was sucked in nearly to my ankle. My left foot was already in motion, and even as I was registering my predicament, it too was sucked in. In my childhood world in Pennsylvania, mud was the stuff you tracked in on your shoes after it rained. It was wet dirt. Messy and oozy and if you were a kid, kinda fun, but it did not kill you. This, to my way of thinking, was not mud, but quicksand, and even with no previous knowledge of it, I knew it was dangerous. I needed help, but there was no one nearby. No one knew where I was. I had nothing to grab for leverage. It was just me, stuck in the mud and utterly terrified I was going to sink deeper. Panicked, I threw myself against the grassy bank, wrapped my fingers in the tall grass and hung on while I pulled with all I was worth. The left foot came free first. I tucked it up beneath me on the bank and fought for the other one. But stuck it stayed. Finally, one hand still wrapped in the grass, I bent over and loosened the laces on the sneaker and pulled my foot free.

I never forgot that mud.

Days passed, and the mystery of J. P. Puglisi continued. Two weeks after he was reported missing, I made the drive north to Long Beach,

Washington, a journey of about 150 miles that took close to four hours. I visited with the Pacific County sheriff's deputies and talked with locals. The report of a man naked or nearly so had caught everyone's attention. No one swam in that water in February, and everyone local knew the mud was dangerous.

Locals theorized that Puglisi had attempted to walk across the mud. About midway, if he made it that far, he would have found himself at a twenty-to-thirty-foot wide current. It was possible that he'd made it across the current and to the island. But once there he would have found a challenging, steep-sided, bramble-covered hike. It was also possible that he waited too long to return and had tried to outrun the incoming tide and nightfall. He may have been weakened by hypothermia; he may have tried swimming and drowned—or he may have been sucked in by the mud. It was a sad story about an intelligent, adventurous man with a playful spirit, and a drive to understand the meaning of life.

It was time to write, but after just eighteen months on the beat, I was already sick of so many nights spent in hotels. So early that afternoon, I made the return trip home, arriving in late afternoon. At my desk, I

Bianca Marthen looks across Willapa Bay where her friend John Puglisi drowned.

signed on to my email. There was a note from an address I didn't recognize. I clicked on it and read: "We are friends of John Puglisi's and will be in Long Beach tomorrow morning." Bianca Marthen had flown in from Indiana with her mother and daughter to see the place that enthralled her best friend and presumably took his life. They'd never been to the Pacific Northwest and had only a vague idea where they were headed. I agreed to meet them. At 6:00 a.m. the next morning, I got up and did it all over again—ultimately logging over seven hundred miles in just three days.

I met Marthen and her family at the parking area across from Baby Island, and learned of a young man who ranked the Pacific Northwest coast as one of the sights he most wanted to see in his life. Three weeks before his thirtieth birthday, he flew here from Indiana. Two days later, his footprints in the mud hinted at his tragic fate.

"He said he had to see the ocean before he turned thirty," Marthen said. "He had this whole list of things he wanted to do. He was so full of life and plans."

Almost a month to the day Puglisi went missing, the tides washed his body onto the mud flats of the Willapa Natural Wildlife Refuge. He died of hypothermia and asphyxiation from drowning.

Julie Herman's death the following month was supposed to look like the result of a house fire. Firefighters found her as they worked to douse the flames in her hillside home in Oceanside. In fact, she'd been murdered. It was the first murder in this little town in twenty-one years. But Oceanside was no stranger to conflict. It was at the time the setting of the ugliest land-use battle I've witnessed anywhere on the coast. It started when a Seattle developer bought the Anchor Tavern, an old former military barracks moved to the spot in 1940, and set about turning it into a boutique hotel with an upscale restaurant. The remodel involved adding a third floor, which blocked the prime ocean view of the homes behind it. Locals and visitors alike were enraged by the blocked views and for what they considered the ruining of a beloved salty old mainstay. Most believed the county had erred in allowing the developer to expand the place and were appealing the decision.

Meanwhile, signs boldly lettered in black and white reading, "Boycott the Anchor," hung from homes all over the hillside, including the sixty-year-old Herman's. It wasn't a pretty sight. The anger in Oceanside was palpable. The developer accused one neighbor of hitting him and called the sheriff. The neighbor said he only sought to get the developer's attention by tapping him on the shoulder as he operated a noisy piece of equipment late one night. But the boycott was working. The Anchor was empty and only one and a half years after the developer bought the place, it was up for sale.

Now Herman, a vocal opponent, was dead, sparking questions, theories, and accusations that only fueled the fire. Was her death related to the boycott? It seemed unlikely, and yet, things had gotten very ugly.

A day after Herman's body was found, deputies arrested Frank Hoyt Pike, twenty-nine. Pike was a construction worker, out of a Virginia prison on parole for the shaking death of his fourteen-week-old son. The motive, it would turn out, was money. Pike was working on a house next to Herman's. She was on the phone with her daughter when Herman told her daughter someone wanted to use her phone and she would call her back. The return call never came. Pike had duct-taped Herman to a chair and stabbed her in the neck. He started the fire to hide the crime and left with a few hundred dollars. He is serving life in prison.

But if the days were dark in this once carefree vacation town, at least one person saw the light. Polish immigrant Sam Piskorski moved to the United States in 1981, first to Las Vegas and then to Oregon where he earned a living as a sheet metal worker. He began investing in property and soon amassed a nice little chunk of money and real estate. When he discovered Oceanside in the mid-1990s, he saw a place, where "you can invest and you are never going to lose."

"I said, 'Wow, I want to live here,'" recalled Piskorski. "I wanted to buy my own tavern. That was my dream."

And so that summer, Piskorski, forty-three, bought the Anchor Inn & Grill. He paid $1.7 million, trading his Oceanside home as part of the down payment. Now the locals could take down their signs. Right? Piskorski was not, after all, the Seattle developer who ruined things. He was a good guy. Even the locals agreed with that. Still, the boycott signs stayed. And while guests wrote glowing reviews of his food, they also told Piskorski they feared patronizing the place. Then one day, one of the staff called Piskorski in Portland to say the propane tanks were empty—even though they'd just been filled. Fearful of a leak or even an explosion, Piskorski closed the restaurant.

Then the propane delivery truck arrived. "The first thing they saw was that someone had shut off my valves," Piskorski said.

Suddenly, Piskorski was beginning to doubt his decision to buy the Anchor.

"I had a pretty hard life," he told me. "Now I have a very good life, but with a bunch of problems. I want to retire here. This is the reason I bought this. I want to live here the rest of my life. I will do whatever it takes, but I don't want to go broke."

Still, the battle continued, and no one was winning. It seemed the only hope for an end was for Piskorski to remove the addition and clear the homeowners' views. But Piskorski said he couldn't do that without losing his shirt. Less than a year after buying it, the embittered investor put it back on the market, this time for $2.4 million.

"People called and canceled reservations because of the boycott," Piskorski said. "People call and ask if it's safe. Then I have to explain to everyone what the boycott is about. I am tired of this. I am really tired of this."

And he was going to get a lot more tired before the Oceanside saga finally ended.

In early November, the winter storms for which the Oregon coast is known were well underway. Gordon McCraw, a meteorologist and Tillamook County Emergency Manager, says Oregon's stormy winters are due largely to the weather systems that form in the Gulf of Alaska and then get pushed southeast by the jet stream, or sometimes move up from the southwest, intensifying as they make landfall. El Niño and La Niña also play a role. Storm seasons generally start in November and stretch through the winter months and even into spring. We didn't know it, but we were coming into a particularly rough couple of years, and McCraw and I would work together often. I'd call him to get a sense of what we were in for, then write the story that sent everyone rushing to the grocery store for supplies. Often storms came in at night, giving me the luxury of riding them out safely at home. Others blew in during the day, and I'd head out, praying to dodge falling trees and whatever other hazards awaited.

That fall, the wind and rain had been raging for days when I learned that two houses on the headlands in Gleneden Beach were perilously close to being pitched to the beach below. I jumped in the RAV and headed that way. Pulling up to the homes, I found a stream of people emptying the house of its contents. A dog sat calmly in his kennel in the garage awaiting transport to safer ground. It was pouring. Absolutely pouring. The water came not in drops or even thunderous showers, but in unbroken, uninterrupted, relentless sheets of water. I wore a light jacket and jeans. After six years on the coast, I still did not possess proper rain gear, and I was about to get soaked. But somehow I had to keep my notebook dry. Once wet, I wouldn't be able to write on it. So I did the only thing I could think of—I shoved it down the front of my jeans.

At the door, one of the friends helping Lynn and Jim Nelson evacuate told me to go on in. Inside, I introduced myself to a woman packing goods into cardboard boxes. She turned out to be homeowner Lynn Nelson. Despite the dire circumstances, she was warm and friendly, though the stress of the situation was obvious. Their home insurance would cover nothing; their flood insurance came with a $250,000 maximum and would not cover the home's contents. "We worked our whole lives to get to this point," Nelson told me as she led me to the second floor for a better look.

As we climbed the stairs, she explained how the summer before, shifting ocean currents had begun eating at the bluffs below. Then a winter storm damaged the bluff allowing the ocean to tunnel beneath it and create caves. Nelson and her neighbors, Carol and Ron Schaaf, knew they were in trouble, but Oregon's strict rules about riprap prevented them from taking action. They fit the criteria that the property had to have been developed before January 1, 1977, but the problem arose with second criteria: the property had to be in imminent danger.

According to Tony Stein, coastal land-use coordinator with Oregon Parks and Recreation, imminent danger means the ocean will cause severe damage to it in the next sixty to ninety days, about the time it takes to get the permit approved.

Nelson didn't apply for a riprap permit when the damage first became obvious because she'd been told by the previous property owner that the house wouldn't be considered in danger until she lost half of the thirty-foot setback. "We knew it was pointless," she said. Days before as she talked on the phone with Ron Schaaf, she watched his hedge disappear from the backyard. Nelson screamed. It wasn't just sloughing, she said. "You heard a boom and it fell."

It was the weekend, and they couldn't reach Stein, the one person who could authorize the permit so they could stabilize the bluff. The two homeowners agreed to sign a blank check to a nearby rock company, which sent trucks loaded with boulders, awaiting the go-ahead from the state. Finally, someone found the home number for Stein, who signed off on the permit.

I followed Nelson to the second floor where she opened the door to a bedroom and directed me to the outside deck. From there, I had a full view of the danger they were facing. Gone were the backyards save for a few feet of the her own. Beyond that was a gaping hole of about sixty feet. Below, heavy equipment operators worked to build a temporary road so the trucks could bring in what would end up being one thousand truckloads of boulders. In the wind and rain, on the edge of seas surging twenty to twenty-five feet, it was the ultimate race against time.

Meanwhile, I had no choice but to go outside on the deck. There were pictures to be taken. And, of course, it was the last place I wanted to be. Once that tiniest bit of remaining yard fell, the house would crumble. Nelson told me to take my time and went back downstairs to finish packing. I threw open the door and stepped out. It was helicopter time all over again, and my knees were instantly knocking. I braced myself against the wind and raised the camera for a shot. But my hands shook, and no amount of bracing myself did one bit of good. If I could just get one or two decent shots. And then, KABOOM. I jumped, shrieking, then saw the wind had slammed the door shut. My first thought as I lunged for the door was, what if I was locked out? I grabbed the doorknob, felt it turn, and pushed my way inside. My photos were lousy and I knew it, but damned if I was going back out there to take more. I was done being brave.

The storm raged on. I raced up to Tillamook and found the city under water, the river raging so high and close to the road, I feared I'd get sucked in. I rolled down my window just in case so I would have a way out. By the time I returned home, it was four in the afternoon. The only thing I'd eaten all day was an energy bar. I still hadn't showered.

By the next morning, the rains had slowed, and there was even a peek of sun, but the storm's toll was still being tallied. The houses on the headland had been saved, but the lives of two women there had not. Elma Benefiel, seventy-eight, of Beaverton, and her daughter-in-law, Jan Benefiel, sixty-one, of Idaho Falls, had offered Depoe Bay Fire Lieutenant Vicky Ryan a cup of coffee before heading out for their morning beach walk. Ryan, stationed at the beach access, had warned them it was no day to be on the beach, but they went anyway. They likely became trapped on the rocks after coming to a stretch of beach made impassable by the surging seas and were washed away by storm waves.

It was a tale I'd end up telling many times—only the names, dates and location changed; the outcome always the same.

A month later, yet another storm blew in, and this one had me a little worried. I'd been here long enough to recognize the signs: the change in the pressure, and yes, the calm before the storm and then soon enough, the inevitable rain, blinding sheets of it; the winds roaring to one hundred miles per hour and more. I told my editor, "You know, I'll probably lose power." To which she replied, "You know, you still have to file a story." I worked all afternoon to get the top of the story written so if I did lose power I would at least have that much. The power started going out around town at 11:00 a.m. and lasted all day into the night. But mine remained on. I turned on the scanner. It was the first time I'd listened to a scanner during a storm, and hearing Chan and his fellow linemen at work as powerlines fell igniting brush fires, and the winds gusted, taking down trees and blowing cars off the road, utterly unnerved me. The house shook and creaked in the wind; rain cracked against the windows. Then came a loud boom, a flash, and then darkness. A transformer had blown up just beyond my office window. I used my cell to call the desk in Portland. A fellow reporter answered and asked, "Can you go out and shoot some photos?"

"There are trees falling down all over the place, and it's a black hole out there," I said. "What exactly do you think I'm going to get a shot of?" Assuming, of course, I wasn't killed by a falling tree or blown away.

I hung up and finished my work, writing by candlelight at the kitchen counter, then dictating the words over my cell phone to my editor in the newsroom. The Coast Guard sent out a message that they had closed the entire coast—the first I'd ever known them to do so. Seas were surging to thirty-five feet. That meant if you were safe in harbor, you stayed and if you were out at sea, you were stuck. By then it was already too late for some.

In the morning, the editors started looking for me at 7:00. There was no power from Gleneden Beach clear to Astoria—nearly a third of the coastline. I headed north and got as far as Neskowin when I realized I didn't have enough gas and there was no hope of getting any farther north. I turned back for Depoe Bay, where I'd seen two open gas stations, but by the time I got back, one station was already sold out and at the other, cars were lined up twelve deep. Now I was on empty. I made a run for Newport and coasted in on fumes to the first gas station I found. All that was left was Supreme. I took it. Back in my office, I filed an update for the web and considered my day done. Then came the message about the beached catamaran and its missing crew.

I found the fifty-foot "Cat Shot" on the beach off Road's End in Lincoln City. The three-man crew had been sailing it from South Africa to Seattle to be delivered to the owner. The cabin had been ripped off. The final entry in the log book showed the crew had been off of Cape Blanco days earlier riding out the storm and were last seen in San Francisco about a week before. Now, the only sign of the crews' struggle was a length of rope dangling from the vessel, a grim reminder, the police officer on site told me, of the crews' efforts to stay with the boat.

FOUR

FINDING THE RHYTHM

2007

I was three years into the beat. I no longer fought nut graphs and I was beginning to get over the sense that I had no idea what I was doing. But I was also growing reclusive. There seemed no way to separate Lori Tobias, reporter for the *Oregonian*, and Lori Tobias, private person who just wanted to be out having fun. People felt perfectly comfortable approaching me at social events with their requests for a story, or complaints of why I hadn't done a story, or criticism of how I'd done a story.

Once at a friend's birthday party, a woman, clearly annoyed, approached me to voice her displeasure that I had quoted someone as saying there was a time when Nye Beach had not felt so safe at night. Why had I written that, she wanted to know? Nye Beach had never felt unsafe to her, so why would I quote someone as saying otherwise?

Another time, while out with friends partying perhaps just a wee bit more than prudent, I walked outside the pub, only to watch a woman rush up to me: "Are you Lori Tobias?"

I missed my anonymity, my privacy, but there's no denying I had great pride in "owning the coast."

By then, I'd covered murders, drownings, landslides, floods, wind storms, falls, and of course, capsizings. For a time, it seemed I just went from one tragedy or disaster to the next. Frequently, there were no survivors to explain just what had gone wrong. But this time, there were, and they were willing to talk to me.

Crosses mark the jetty at Tillamook Bay bar, where numerous boats have capsized.

It was another capsizing on Tillamook Bay bar, my third and not my last. Locals believe the bar is dangerous because it hasn't been dredged since 1976, and sediments have created a horseshoe-shaped shoal that makes the channel shallower. But the United States Army Corps of Engineers, the agency responsible for dredging, insists the bar is already deeper than the eighteen feet at which it's authorized to dredge. The struggle between the Port of Garibaldi and the Corps has stretched on for years, if not decades.

This capsizing was of the fifty-eight-foot Starrigavan, slammed by a succession of twenty-plus foot waves as it attempted to cross the bar at 9:30 on the night of January 25. The skipper had just enough time to radio for help before two more waves hit the boat, rolling the steel-hauled vessel three times. I got word of it the next morning and tracked two of the survivors to the hospital where one of the men was still being treated and another was keeping him company. When they agreed to see me, I jumped in the RAV and raced north to Tillamook. A photographer headed in from Portland to meet me. It should have been easy. But I arrived to find a group of Coast Guard officers in the room. A man at the door identified himself as a border patrol agent and stopped me. That there was a border patrol agent in Tillamook, far, far from any foreign border, was odd in itself, though I would later learn that the Coast Guard had been moved under the jurisdiction of the US Department of Homeland Security.

"You can't go in there," he said.

"I've talked to them on the phone; they want to talk to me," I said.

Arms crossed over his chest, he shook his head. About then, I caught survivor Sam Johnson's eye. I made a point of calling out loudly to him. "Hey Sam, just wanted to let you know I'm here. I'm happy to wait until they finish up."

The border patrol agent gave me the evil eye. I ignored him and walked down the hall to sneak a call to the photographer to tell him not to come in. I figured I could wait them out, but two of us would no doubt amp up the authority issue, and we wouldn't win. I parked myself by a window to wait. It wasn't long before Mr. Border Patrol advanced down the hall toward me. I knew he could make my life difficult. All he had to do was tell the nurses not to let me in, and they wouldn't. I also knew his type—a little flattery would go a long way.

So, I smiled at him in that guileless kind of way.

"Beautiful day, huh," I said, gesturing out the window to the blue sky.

"Sure is," he said. "Too bad we're stuck in here."

And so began the small talk. Me, playing the casual, somewhat bored reporter, eager only to get on with her weekend. He, the important man of the law, burdened with the responsibility of keeping silly females like me safe. After a bit of talk about the weather and his long drive to and from Portland, it occurred to me that if they thought I was gone, they might hurry it up a bit.

"You know, I think I'll go get myself some lunch," I said. Then added, "Maybe I'll just talk to them another time."

"Probably a good idea," he said. "By the way, I recommend the cinnamon roll."

"Oh, all those calories," I said. "I don't dare."

"Well if you don't mind me saying," he said. "I think you look wonderful just the way you are."

I gave him a cheery little wave and hurried off. I found the photographer parked outside, and climbed in his pickup, about one row back from where the Coast Guard car was parked. I suggested we move farther away so they didn't see us when they came out. He drove to a spot where we had a good view of the hospital front doors and the Coast Guard truck, but were also tucked between other cars. And there we sat. It was already early afternoon. Once we finally did talk to the guys, if we finally did get to talk to the guys, I still had to drive ninety minutes home. I still had to write the story. The day was already long, and technically I wasn't even on the clock.

Fifteen minutes passed, and I was beginning to wonder if they were ever going to come out. After another ten, they finally appeared. I grabbed my sunglasses and slid farther down in the seat. We watched them walk to the car. Of course, they couldn't just get in and go, they had to stand around and bullshit first. That went on for another five to ten minutes.

Finally, they climbed in and slowly left the parking lot. Just to be on the safe side, I suggested to the photographer that we walk in close together, like any happy couple, the camera hidden between us. Casually, we slipped down the hallway. A nurse glanced up, then away, and we hurried to the room.

Crew members Sam Johnson, thirty-nine, and Gregory Phillips, twenty-three, were pissed. They blamed the captain, Kirk Opheim, twenty-three, who had also survived and who they accused of using meth. (Opheim was later tried on a variety of charges including criminally negligent homicide and second-degree manslaughter, as well as boating under the influence, but found guilty only of the first.) That anyone had survived was just plain luck. And no one deserved more credit for that luck than the man who made it, a young rescue swimmer, who, until that night, had never rescued a soul in his life.

"He took a beating like I've never seen before," Johnson said. "He just wouldn't give up. He kept telling us, 'You guys are going to be okay. I'm here, you are going to make it.'"

The next day I tracked down the swimmer.

On the night the waves wrecked the Starrigavan on the jetty rocks, twenty-two-year-old newlywed Rob Emley's only rescue mission had been by boat, when flooded streets had made roads impassable. "I went up and knocked on people's doors and said, 'Do you guys need a ride?'" he said.

Emley became a rescue swimmer largely because nothing else stuck. After graduating high school, he figured he'd take a break and work for a while. It didn't take too long before he realized the life of a laborer wasn't for him. So, he enrolled in college, but that didn't suit him, either. Then he remembered seeing an ad for the Coast Guard. So he stopped by and talked to the recruiter. Emley grew up in Southern California where he'd spent the better part of his life in the water. A career as a rescue swimmer was an obvious choice—though, as anyone who has seen the *Guardian* knows—not one easily obtained. But Emley, it turned out, was a natural.

"What drew me to the rescue swimmer program was being in the water and being the link between the Coast Guard and the people who need help," he said. "Being that last link."

This is how Emley described his training:

"Wake up early, stretch, take a shower, eat breakfast. I had to be at the workout course, they called it the grinder, at 6:45. You stretch as a class and then the instructors come out, and you work out for roughly two hours on land and then from there you have fifteen minutes to get to the pool. You're in the pool, working out for about another two hours, and you get an hour lunch, sometimes. We tried to slam something light, like a ham sandwich or a bagel with turkey and cheese. We'd have to be back in the pool at 12:30 for another four hours of workout and instruction. That was three days a week, the other two days are all classroom. We would usually go for a run, like a light jog for thirty minutes. It's pretty grueling. I graduated May 5, 2005."

On the night the distress call came from the Starrigavan fishing vessel, 6-foot 1-inch, 210-pound Emley was hanging out with his wife in the duty room. He shut off the coffee pot and grabbed his gear. But even as he rushed to get out the door, he expected to be called back at any moment. The boat crew from Tillamook always beat them to the scene, and the Astoria-based helicopter crew acts as back up, a last resort, Emley said. But that January night, it was too dangerous for the boat.

From the chopper, Emley didn't think the situation on the rocks looked too bad. As far as he could tell, the crew might have just stepped off the vessel onto the jetty. But when he got down on deck, it was "a completely different story."

When the waves hit, they ripped the survival suits from the men's hands and rolled the boat twice, tossing gear and entangling the men in wire and lines. To add to his troubles, Emley wore rubber boots, and just keeping his footing on the wet, nearly vertical deck was a challenge. The crew was trapped in the cabin, where Opheim, Johnson, and Phillips were huddled around Ken "Skinny" Venard, age fifty.

"They were pretty hysterical and rightly so," Emley said. The boat was high centered on the jetty and rocking hard in the waves. Venard was badly injured. He had severe hypothermia and couldn't use his legs. Something big had fallen on Venard. Emley suspected he'd broken his pelvis.

"I started trying to move him out, moving him over the debris on deck," Emley said. "It took me awhile of getting the hang of waiting for the wave to hit, grabbing something, waiting for the boat to stop moving, then moving things. We were moving but not making much progress. It was really tough going. I had his upper body. Sam had his legs. We got him to the top of the boat, the highest point on the boat, where it was out in the open, but sheltered from the waves. I signaled for the basket with hand signals. They had a spotlight on us the whole time. The pilot and flight mechanic did a perfect job. They lowered a trail line so I could reel in the basket. I pulled in the rope and guided the basket onto the deck. They kept the basket from swinging and made it land in the right spot. That's when the first big wave hit. It washed me and Skinny from the top of the deck to the other end."

Now, Emley had to drag Venard back across the deck, tilted at about thirty degrees, around the debris and back to the basket. Sitting on the deck, he wrapped his arms around Venard, who wore only a shirt and socks, and, using his feet to push, inched the two of them across the deck. Emley may not have acted like a man who was scared, but he was. Any wave could easily roll the boat on its top, trapping them all underneath.

Finally, he and Venard were back at the cabin.

"I said, 'We're going to do it this time.' I was starting to get the rhythm of the way the ocean was working. A wave would hit and you had maybe five to ten seconds to work before there came another huge impact. If you weren't bracing yourself, it completely wiped away everything you were working for. It was one step forward, two back.

"Meanwhile, as all this is going on, the pilot and flight mechanic were keeping the basket on the deck without having the cable get wrapped around anything. They did an awesome job. The helicopter is holding a hover. I thought about taking the basket off the hook. I didn't want them to get fouled up and have to sheer the cable because then where would we be?

"At that point, it was a pretty dangerous spot. If the boat went down and the helicopter went up, it would pull that cable taut. You're not going to hold onto a basket if the helicopter was pulling it up. A person isn't anything. It doesn't matter how strong you are."

Finally, Venard was safely into the helicopter. Emley shouted for the next person and saw the men gesture toward the sky. He turned to see the helicopter flying away. Venard was too bad off to wait. (He later died at the hospital.) Ten minutes later, the crew was back, and Emley went to work getting the other men to safety.

"The younger guy said, 'This is my first season . . . my first time out . . . my first everything.' I said, 'Me, too.' He just looked at me, 'Oh, that makes me feel better.' That's what he said to me."

Emley got the others loaded, then waited for his turn, just him, the sea, the stars, and one wrecked boat. He'd been on the vessel about one hour.

"I remember looking out after I got that last guy up. I was sitting there watching these waves come in. I had gotten a rhythm. I felt secure. It was almost a comfortable feeling."

It was a dark spring. Three soldiers with Newport ties were lost in two short months. In those days, the *Oregonian* covered every death, and I found myself going from one service to another.

My brother Jerry had served in Vietnam. He went off when I was eight. A patriotic, happy, can-do kind of guy, fresh out of high school, Jerry came home from his service as a riverboat patrolman, angry, uneasy and mostly antisocial. There were moments when Jerry would seem almost like the young man he was before serving his country, but eventually that happy soul would fade behind anger and unease. He died at sixty-four from a diseased liver, brought on by alcohol and, likely, Agent Orange. No one ever diagnosed or treated him (he wouldn't have anything to do with the VA or government), but in hindsight it is obvious he battled PTSD nearly all of his life. I think my brother, as well as my dad, a Korean War vet who was drafted and came home with two Purple Hearts, gave me a certain empathy, bond even, to those young men who were going—and often not coming back.

One of the young men who died that spring was my hairdresser's step-son. Nick Lightner was a twenty-nine-year-old medic on patrol in Baghdad when a land mine exploded. Despite injuries of his own, including a broken leg and a stomach pierced with shrapnel, Lightner worked to save the life of a fellow soldier. Four died on the scene, a fifth died three days later in the hospital. Lightner was transferred to the Walter Reed Army Medical Center in Washington, DC. His injuries were serious, but he was expected to survive. Yet six days after the attack, Lightner died.

His family told me about the chaplain who had sat with Lightner, comforting him and talking with him while his family was en route. I was always in awe of that chaplain. What greater kindness could someone offer a stranger? That spring, I would offer the only comfort I knew, to share the stories of these young men: the high points of their lives, the good others remembered, their passions, the moments that brought them joy.

At one service in Newport, the stepmother kicked me out. My editor asked if they'd allowed other members of the media inside. If so, they had to let me in. I told her the truth. I didn't know if other reporters were there, but it was a funeral, and I wasn't pushing my way in for any reason. Afterward, however, the father of the dead soldier was surprised to hear I had been banned and asked if someone would please cover the service being held later in Portland.

Sometimes, the family is too grief-stricken to talk. So you find others who can help paint the picture of that singular life. I've found friends at the local grocery store. I've called recruiting officers, the high school. I've talked with in-laws, exes, old babysitters.

But the Lightners wanted to talk about Nick. I talked to his dad, his brother and, of course, his stepmom, Sheri. When we finished talking, Sheri asked me to call Sharon Branstiter, the mayor of Toledo. I had never spoken to Branstiter, but I knew her reputation as a no-nonsense woman who always got the job done. She was a retired high school counselor and close to Lightner's family.

Branstiter got back to me as I was driving. I pulled over, and pulled out the only pad of paper on hand, a small black Moleskin I kept in my purse for random notes, ideas, and shopping lists. Then, she insisted everything was off the record until she was sure she could trust me, which normally, she said, she would not have even considered. But having read an earlier story I'd written about another fallen soldier, she decided to give me a chance. Plus, there were things she wanted people to know about Lightner.

She laid out some ground rules. There were details she would share about Lightner just so I would understand his full nature, but I was not under any circumstances to include them in the story. Did we understand each other? We did. In that case, she was ready to talk. I listened as she spoke, until we agreed she was on the record. My pen flew over the five-and-a-half-inch ruled sheet of paper, moving from one page to the next in the reporter's shorthand I'd developed over the years. Branstiter talked about a young man who was kind and compassionate, a high school football player who would be a friend to anyone, and who was a son to many. He'd enlisted after 9/11 because he wanted to do something, to make a difference.

A few days later, I attended Lightner's funeral, where Branstiter spoke to the standing-room only crowd. When the service was over, I introduced myself. Branstiter, a stout woman with a warm smile, reached out and hugged me. She thanked me for doing a fine job. It seemed to me I'd been tested and passed, and I was proud of that.

Three weeks later, I was at my desk when I got news of Branstiter's death. She'd died at home while recovering from double bypass surgery. She was sixty-three.

A year and a half had passed since the effort to make life jackets on charter boats mandatory had failed. It was one of those stories that is all over the headlines and then quietly disappears. But it was still recent enough, controversial enough, to remain fresh in people's minds. And it was, of course, the first thing that came to mind for many upon hearing that Jim "Bear" Edson had died while fishing off of Waldport on a Saturday afternoon in May. I learned about it Sunday morning and headed for the docks on Yaquina Bay where Edson kept his *Three Bears* charter boat. But all was quiet, and I decided to give it up and go home to enjoy my Sunday. As I climbed the ramp to the parking lot, a man and woman passed me. She was crying, and I could make out enough of their conversation to realize they knew Edson.

I introduced myself. The woman was Edson's girlfriend, and she was livid at a TV reporter who suggested that Edson might be alive if he'd been wearing a life jacket. It wasn't true, she insisted, and she was hopeful I could set the record straight. Out came the notebook. She railed, I wrote, saying nothing, of course, of my own suspicions. Maybe it was true that a life jacket could not have saved him, but the irony. You couldn't escape the irony.

Casey Roberts was on the boat with Edson that day. He had just hooked a halibut about fifteen miles west of Waldport. Edson, whose nickname reflected his 6-foot 2-inch, 300-pound size, was helping Roberts pull it onboard. Roberts turned his back, then turned again, just as Edson flipped over the rail.

"Pull me up, guys. Pull me up," Roberts heard him call.

Someone on the boat threw Edson a life ring, and Roberts and two other men tried to pull him from the water back onto the boat. But Edson was too heavy for the men. Roberts donned a life jacket and dove in. Edson was still coherent, but Roberts couldn't help. The other passengers helped Roberts back onto the boat. Moments later, Edson was dead. He'd been in the water only five minutes.

An autopsy later showed that Edson had died by asphyxiation due to drowning and that hypothermia had contributed to his death. Would a life jacket have done any good? We'll never know.

In June, we began hearing about the couple who had never checked out of their Portland hotel room. The couple, David Schwartz, fifty-two, and Cheryl Gibbs, sixty-one, were by all accounts good friends only. He was a Jesuit priest; she worked for the Alameda County Coroner's office. The two were said to share a love of travel. They were last seen at the hotel on June 8. Their luggage and belongings were left in the hotel room. There was no sign of struggle or foul play. A hotel clerk said Schwartz and Gibbs mentioned they were going to visit Multnomah Falls and attend Rose Festival events. And then, it seemed they had simply vanished.

Three weeks later on a Friday afternoon, Tillamook County Sheriff Todd Anderson called to say that family members who'd come up from California to try to find the couple had discovered Gibbs's signature in the guestbook of the Tillamook Cheese Factory. The search was on. I called the desk to let them know and wrote up a quick brief. Saturday morning, I drove to Tillamook, waiting and watching as the volunteers with the Civil Air Patrol (CAP) came and went from the local airport, while nine volunteer search and rescue teams scoured the rugged landscape. I assumed they would find them at any moment, but the morning came and went and soon it was afternoon, and not a sign of the pair. I headed home and made some phone calls around Tillamook. I talked to a woman at a café where the two had had coffee. I talked to Melissa Stetzel at the Nehalem Bay Winery. The couple had been there to sample wine and had bought a bottle. That seemed to be the final clue. Maybe they had taken the winding Oregon 53 or the gravel Foss Road, described by Anderson as a very scenic route but with blind curves and steep drop offs.

By Sunday, they still had not been found. Then, late that afternoon a Civil Air Patrol pilot spotted the maroon Toyota Corolla wrecked just off of Highway 26, hidden from sight in the dense brush. They were not wearing seatbelts and had likely died on impact.

My work mostly ended there, but the story did not. My colleagues in Portland learned there had been a phone call to report an accident. But deputies did not find the wreckage at the time. The caller apparently gave the emergency dispatch a bogus number and was never located—leaving one to wonder what role his vehicle might have played in the crash.

In the fall, I returned to Denver for the first time since leaving in 2000. I was part of a discussion at the Denver Woman's Press Club about the state of journalism. Spirits among my fellow journalists were low, and I realized how lucky I was. Things didn't seem nearly so bad in Oregon. The *Rocky* had moved from the building I'd worked in and now shared a towering office building with the *Denver Post*. The *Rocky* had the lower floors with the *Post* occupying the top floors and security guards posted to ensure reporters from one paper did not slip into rival territory. When I visited the *Rocky* newsroom, it was largely deserted, and I later noted in my journal that the paper was "pretty lifeless." It was great seeing my friends, though I didn't get to talk with everyone, something I would come to regret very soon.

But what stuck with me most about that visit was a brief exchange with managing editor John Temple. He was in the daily "budget" meeting—the planning meeting for the next day's paper—but stepped out for a moment. He greeted me with a hug, and said, "You have a great beat in Oregon. There must be a book in it."

Indeed.

Back home, I was on tap to write the A1 Monday profile—and it was killing me. The subject was Ray Shackelford, owner of the Nehalem Bay Winery, and as complex a man as I'd met. I'd learned about Shackelford after receiving an email sharing the news of his work in Cambodia, where he'd helped build schools and a sewing room. The villagers make silk-like wine bags, backpacks, and handbags, and Shackelford sells them at the winery, then sends the proceeds back to the village.

I visited with Shackelford at the winery, ran errands with him in his pick up, and continued the conversation online and by phone. By the time I sat down to write, I had twenty-three pages of notes—7,882 words, and no idea what to do with it. Worse, I was in the midst of a home remodel and crews worked beneath my office with seemingly every loud, vibrating, floor-shaking power tool known to man.

I was having such a hard time, I reached out to the *Oregonian*'s writing coach Jack Hart for help. It was the first time I had a one-on-one with Hart, and I was eager for his wisdom. But when his call came, the workers below fired up the jackhammer, and I don't think I heard more than a dozen words in the whole fifteen-minute conversation.

When stuck, I had a couple of different tactics. Sometimes, after reading and rereading my notes, after one false lede (the newsroom spelling of lead, which I learned through numerous Internet sources, came about way back in the day to avoid confusion with the word lead, as in hot molten lead used in typesetting) after another after another, I'd walk away from my desk and let it go. I'd do the dishes or dust or go for a walk and often as not, there it would be, as obvious as if written in the sky. And once I knew my lede, the rest would generally fall into place. My other approach was to sit quietly, to meditate, at least to the degree that my mind ever quiets enough for that to truly happen.

But even after I had my lede for Shackelford, a lede I liked, I fought it.

His stories almost defied belief, and sometimes as I listened I felt a niggling of worry, which I mostly ignored. By the age of twenty-five, he'd married and divorced, spent a short time in a Cuban Army prison after signing on to help Castro win the revolution. After losing his draft card in Mexico, he went by the draft office for a new one and thirty days later found himself with an invitation from Uncle Sam. He spent three and a half years in Vietnam, caught two bullets, and severely damaged his ears after a grenade landed in his bunker and he tossed it away. He was wounded by a punji stake—a bamboo or wood stake used as a booby trap of sorts—and went home with two Silver Stars.

He talked of his first visit back to Vietnam twenty years after he left.

"Quite a few times, I almost hyperventilated," Shackelford told me. "I literally walked down the same trail where I triggered an ambush on a North Vietnamese Army Officer and his lover. He was hit first, and she went down and held his head to her heart until they were both killed."

He talked of being robbed in Sisophon, Cambodia, and of an encounter with Ieng Sary, a senior member and cofounder of the Khmer Rouge. Shackelford was traveling with "Elephant," a friend he'd met in Cambodia who happened to be from the same village where Shackelford had served as a senior advisor to an artillery battalion.

"I had heard Ieng Sary lived there in Piland," Shackelford said. "The people told me where it was. I said, 'Let's go look at his house. I'll take a picture. Just a tourist.' Elephant didn't talk. He was really, really nervous. His family had been killed. At that exact time, two guys walked out of the house. I yelled, 'Can I take a picture?' Elephant said, 'That's Ieng Sary.' He was with his secretary. The secretary spoke almost perfect English. He said, 'Come on in and have tea. Please have tea.' And so the guards opened up the gate and Elephant and I walked in. The guards patted us down, and we had tea. I said, 'You were involved with Khmer Rouge at that time, isn't that right?' And he said, 'I don't talk about that period of my life.' He showed me a piece of paper, an invitation to a Buddhist ceremony that he was sponsoring. I said I won't be able to be there. I reached in my pocket and got out a twenty-dollar bill and said I would like to support the ceremony. The secretary took the money. Ieng Sary wouldn't take it."

Shackelford talked of his childhood, of getting the beating of his life by his dad after bringing an African American boy to their Oklahoma home. Shackelford is a conservative, with leanings toward Libertarianism, and a strong inclination to question authority. He is known in the community for his charity, the music festivals he promotes and sponsors. Once, he had the lumberyard deliver plywood so there would be place to dance at a concert in the park.

I talked to employees who credited him with helping them raise their children, pay their mortgages, and manage their money so they could afford medication. They also spoke of a man who could be demanding, but believed in second chances.

Shackelford told me of his travels, of his lifelong desire not to live some typical life behind a white picket fence. He told me, too, about his habit of getting up at night and going for a drive.

"When I get up and go out to the truck I don't know why I do it, I just know that I do," he wrote in one of his emails, some which came in all capital letters, others in all lower case. "Some shrink once said that it was a continuation of being in Vietnam and getting up and checking the perimeter. So I just get up and look around, go to the truck and sometimes drive up the river or to the beach or sometimes just move the truck and sleep for a while. Sometimes it's all night and sometimes just for a short time. I have been awakened by the person opening the tasting room more than once, but they know I am not the normal average guy so it's not a surprise to them."

After much agonizing, I finally wrangled the Shackelford story into shape. It ran as the Monday A1 centerpiece accompanied by a beautiful

The Oregonian'*s A1 profile of Ray Shackelford. Photo by Melissa Stetzel.*

shot of Shackelford by my colleague Stephanie Yao. Almost immediately the phone calls and emails flowed in, all congratulating me on a "great job." I could have hardly been prouder.

Then came the email from a marine I'll call Dale. Dale not only questioned if Shackelford had truly earned two Silver Stars, but if he'd even been in Vietnam. It seemed Dale had once met Shackelford at the winery, and the white-bearded, blue-eyed man bearing a certain resemblance to a tanned Santa did not strike Dale as officer material.

Instantly, I felt my stomach turn. I had been drawn to profile Shackelford largely due to reports of his philanthropic efforts, and now there was a possibility he'd lied? While I'd had my concerns, for the most part I trusted Shackelford. I'd met him; I'd met his employees and interviewed numerous friends. It never occurred to me to check his story through the military. I called my editors. They agreed, it was worrisome, and we needed to have our researchers check it out. I called Shackelford, who sounded puzzled, but calm, and assured me it would all work itself out. Meanwhile, the guy who'd emailed me planned to launch his own investigation.

I wrote my editor to ask how badly it would bode for me if it turned out Dale was right.

"Relax," he wrote. "We've all been snookered by sources."

Four days later, I received another note from Dale. He said he believed he owed me an apology. In the end, Shackelford's story proved true and it remains one of my favorite profiles.

I had been planning to write about Terrible Tilly for months, but there was always something more important. Then, I got wind that the *New York Times* was planning a story. It pained the hell out of me that a newspaper from back East—never mind it was the *New York Times*—might beat me to a story on my own beat. I went to work.

Terrible Tilly is the name given the lighthouse perched on Tillamook Rock, about one mile west of Tillamook Head. Built in the 1800s, it was considered the engineering feat of its day—no doubt in large part due to the brutal conditions under which it was constructed. Because of the toll it took on lighthouse keepers and laborers, the lighthouse went dark in 1957 and changed hands numerous times.

In 1979, Mimi Morissette and other investors purchased Tilly for $50,000, dubbed it Eternity at Sea, and repurposed it as a columbarium. For a cost of $1,000 to $5,000, individuals could arrange to have their cremains stored in the oft photographed, reportedly haunted lighthouse at sea. Plans called for 300,000 urns to be stored there. One of those was to be Martha McDaid's. Granddaughter Katharine Brendle described her grandmother as a tiny redhead who once dreamed of being an actress and imagined her cremains in the company of many movie stars. Martha saved from her Social Security check to come up with the $1,500 tab, and in 1981 purchased her niche at Eternity at Sea. She hung the framed print from Eternity at Sea and mused about the place her remains would occupy there. It was all very glamorous to her, Brendle said.

But in 1999, the Eternity at Sea owners failed to renew their license to operate the columbarium and in 2005, the Oregon Mortuary and Cemetery Board denied the new one. There were reportedly thirty-two urns stored in Terrible Tilly's sixty-two-foot tall tower. And then thirty, after two had been reported missing when the lighthouse was vandalized. The columbarium, now part of the Oregon Islands National Wildlife Refuge, has largely been overtaken by seabirds.

I finished writing my story, breathing a sigh that I had not been beat by that other paper. It would run the next day. That's when my editor called. "Call it a day," he said. There was not enough space for the story, and it would have to hold. You can guess what I found in the *New York Times* the next morning. My story ran in the *Oregonian* the day after.

And what of Martha McDaid's cremains? All these years later, Brendle knows only that, before the columbarium license was revoked, the mortuary delivered her grandmother's ashes to the art gallery owned by one of the investors in Eternity at Sea. The owners promised to see to it that the cremains were taken out to the lighthouse on one of the twice-annual flights to Tilly. Whether or not McDaid got the special urn with the engraved nameplate, much less made it to the lighthouse, Brendle has no idea. Messages to Eternity at Sea have gone unanswered.

"It haunts me," Brendle said when we spoke recently. "It was my Dad's dying wish, 'Please make sure your Grandmother makes it out there.' They were going to send me pictures. I never heard another thing."

More than a year had passed since Sam Piskorski put the Anchor Tavern back on the market. By the fall of 2007, he was angry, but, even more so, desperate. I liked Piskorski, and I understood his anger; he was losing everything. I liked some of the Oceanside neighbors I met through the story, as well, and I understood their anger at losing their view. But it also seemed to me that the ugliness was ruining the very soul of this once peaceful town. There would be no winners. Now, as the winter storms once again battered the coast, Piskorksi turned to plan B, a sort of middle finger gesture to the locals who continued the boycott. If he couldn't find success running a nice wholesome family operation, he'd try a different approach. The Anchor would become a strip joint. I pulled into town as the winds whipped the rain, and ocean waves swelled and crashed. The street was deserted save for a skinny, pig-tailed girl I watched dash through the rain from the tavern to her quarters upstairs in the formerly chic boutique hotel room. Inside the former upscale restaurant, I found a stage, flashing red lights, darkened windows, and private rooms for lap dances. Piskorski seemed quite pleased with himself.

It was not, however, a laughing matter to the good people of Tillamook County, whose lives tend to revolve around farming, family, dory fishing, and all the outdoor recreation you expect to find in a sweeping landscape of forest, ocean, dunes, and mountain. It was not a place you expect to find strip joints. And yes, I couldn't help grinning as I imagined the stories concocted by the men seeking an excuse to sneak out, allegedly to the grocery or hardwood store. (Hey honey, just discovered I'm a few screws short, be right back.)

The neighbors and visitors alike were beyond pissed. Piskorski held his ground.

"I've got three kids," he said. "I am going to lose one million bucks. I would ask anyone, 'If you were going to lose everything you worked hard for for twenty years, would you do it?' No one would just walk away and say, 'Okay, I lost $1 million.'"

In the end, the bank foreclosed on it. The building was turned into offices and a small café with barely a hint of the old salty Anchor to be seen—nor, with the exception of the additional view-blocking floors, the once-chic boutique hotel.

FIVE

ONE PRESIDENT, TWO CATS, AND A VERY BLACK FRIDAY

2008

For as long as I'd been part of the *Rocky Mountain News*, there had been rumors that Scripps Howard would shut it down. In the early years, we worried about the *Rocky* losing the newspaper war to the *Denver Post*, which in 2000, it did. The two papers formed a Joint Operating Agreement (JOA) with both publishing five days a week, and the *Rocky* publishing the Saturday paper and the *Post*, the Sunday. It was generally considered the paper that did not publish the Sunday edition was the "loser," which was precisely what a columnist at the *Post* called us. After that, the question was how long both papers could survive under the JAO. I had been gone from the *Rocky* longer than I'd been there, but it always felt like the career version of a home town; the place that helped shape me as a journalist. Now, the talk was that Scripps was trying to sell the *Rocky* and they were no longer just unfounded rumors, but credible concerns.

Meanwhile, the *Oregonian* posted sixty job openings, and reporters in Portland and the suburban bureaus were required to apply for the jobs they wanted. No one in the business felt safe.

If that wasn't enough to make life stressful, I'd recently landed a new editor, whose work style was entirely different from that of my old editor. Whereas before I was in touch with the desk several times a day, generally more, this editor didn't want to hear from me but a couple of times a week. When we did talk, he was frequently brusque and impatient. To his credit, he was a stickler for me not working more hours than I was paid and would often tell me to shut down the computer, or take a couple days off. But where once my stories had consistently landed on A1 or the metro cover, more and more often they were being buried inside or on the back page. Given the state of the business, that made me jumpier than ever. I always figured as long as I was landing on A1 or the Metro cover, I had some modicum of job security. There would come a day when I would record every single cover story and add them up at the end of the year. Written reassurance, I guess, that I was earning my keep.

In the end, however, it is not the cover stories or the kudos on a job well done or even the prizes that stay with you nearly so much as knowing you made a difference, helped someone. And I like to think the story I wrote about hunger and homelessness in Lincoln County did that. At the time, 19.1 percent of the Lincoln County population was considered to be living in poverty. In 2008, that was defined as a family of three living on $17,600 or less. Rent at the time averaged $800 a month.

I didn't grow up poor. On the contrary, I had pretty much everything I needed. My parents were not well off, but solidly middle class, and essentially every hour they labored was to provide for us, and then some. But my mother had grown up so poor she quit school at fourteen because she was ashamed of her sole-flapping shoes and ragged clothing. At the age of eighteen, on my own in Anchorage, I learned first-hand how hard it is to live on minimum wage. I was evicted from my first apartment and would have ended up under some bridge had it not been for good friends. Strangers helped, too.

My years as an impoverished college student did not last long, but no period in my life left a bigger mark on my spirit. I'm sure that's part of why I always worried about losing my job. I'm sure it's also why I hand out cash and buy sandwiches for the people on street corners. I have never forgotten how quickly abundance can turn to lack.

I'd been hearing stories about poverty on the coast since moving here. When people think of the coast, they think of the beach and hotels, ocean-front mansions, and all that goes with a tourist destination. Less obvious or perhaps just more comfortably overlooked are the huge numbers of homeless and hungry. It was time for me to write that story.

On a Saturday, I drove to Waldport, where I met for the first time

Senitila McKinley, one of the county's most vocal, invested, involved advocates for the homeless. Lincoln County commissioner Bill Hall, who has since transitioned from male to female and is now Claire Hall, and who is also a tireless advocate for the homeless, dubbed McKinley "The Mother Teresa of Lincoln County."

McKinley, a native of Tonga who came to the United States after meeting her Waldport-native husband Dave while he vacationed in her homeland, founded the Seaside Family Literacy Project and the Community Learning Center. She operated both out of an old school where McKinley took in clothing and household items to give to those in need. Every Saturday, she hosted a Saturday morning breakfast and during the week, after-school snacks. The list of what McKinley has done for those in need would fill a book on its own.

On that Saturday at breakfast, I met a woman who had cancer of the uterus and lived in a travel trailer at a state park. I met another who told me when her mother died, she went a bit crazy and gave away everything she had, and now had nothing. The center was filled with tables and chairs and at each one sat a person grateful for a meal. The food was cooked and served by community volunteers, who then also did the cleanup. As I was leaving, McKinley watched a woman walk to her car. "Do you have enough gas to make it home?" McKinley called.

"I hope so," the woman answered. "Probably not."

McKinley excused herself, walked to her car, rifled around some boxes and bags, and emerged with several folded bills. "Here," she said. "I just happened to have this in my car. It's your lucky day."

Later in the week, I drove north to Lincoln City to visit Oceanlake Elementary School, where three-quarters of the student body qualified for free or reduced lunch. Minutes before school was to let out, I listened from a counselor's office as the announcement came over the speaker: "Just a friendly reminder. It's backpack Friday." Soon, a cluster of first and second graders rushed into the office, each hefting a backpack filled with fourteen dollars' worth of food, including a loaf of bread, peanut butter and jelly, tins of tuna or other meat, macaroni and cheese, fruit and juice — all of it donated or purchased with donations and packed, stuffed, and otherwise handled by volunteers. When the program started the year before, five children took home packs. Now, there were seventy-five students in Lincoln City's three schools relying on Backpack Friday to get them through the weekend, when they otherwise might not get much to eat. Often, the backpacks also held extra for older siblings at home. I'd tried for days to find a parent who would speak to me about the program, but it seemed the shame of needing help was too great.

My story ran on the top of the fold on the Monday Metro cover and the deluge started. People emailed and called and every single one of them wanted to help. In Portland, the newsroom also took calls. And they continued for days.

Weeks later, four reporters announced their plans to leave the *Oregonian*, including the editor who hired me. I went to Portland for his goodbye party and told him my concerns about my job. He laughed. "They'd have to be crazy to let you go," he said. "What is Oregon without the coast?" I thought if anyone would know, it was this guy. I breathed easier. Just a little. Still, when a reporter in Portland asked me to drop everything to drive twenty miles north for a photo for her story, I didn't even think of saying no. I told myself the more indispensable I was, the better the odds of dodging the bullets that seemed to come ever more frequently.

But when a plane crashed into a rental house in Gearhart, my editor was out and the breaking news team hustled off to do the story while I watched from home, feeling cut out of my own turf. It seemed to be happening more and more often, and I didn't know what to do about it. A week later, I got an email from my editor with a phone number to call. I pieced together enough to know I would be calling someone about a double fatality. But who? I asked the editor for more details.

"Lori, just call the goddamned number," he said. I was beginning to sincerely despise the guy—and my job. As it turned out, that number belonged to the stepfather of a young man and his wife who were struck in the wee hours of the morning by a drunk driver as they stood arguing by a back country road.

That spring Chan and I celebrated our twenty-fifth anniversary with a long-awaited Mediterranean cruise. We'd been home only one day, and though technically I was back on the clock, I was planning to stretch vacation mode a bit longer. But at noon my editor called to say Bill Clinton was coming to town to stump for Hillary, and I needed to attend. Jet lagged and in a fog, I slapped on some makeup, slipped into jeans and a pair of Crocs, and headed to the Port of Newport, where he was due at 3:30 p.m. I wouldn't need to write anything—unless something unexpected happened. I headed for the port early, as I often do when covering an event like that. It's an old habit adopted largely to give me time to study the lay of the land and to make sure I find a good place from which to take it all in. Somehow my addlepated brain had failed to fully appreciate what a visit from a former twice-elected president would mean to this little county of roughly forty-six thousand. I arrived to find what looked like half of Lincoln County lined up for tickets. I didn't know how many people could be accommodated, but as I took my place at the end of a very long line, I thought there was a good chance I wouldn't even get in. It seemed there was nothing to do but wait and see and hope for the best.

Then turning, I saw the press box atop a flatbed. Ha, of course. I was a member of the press. My seat was right there, reserved, even. I found the press coordinator and claimed my front-row folding chair on the still empty flatbed. I was not alone for long. Soon I was joined not only by the local press but also by what appeared to be every secretary, salesman, and bean counter from every media outlet in the county. This was clearly the event of the decade, and I seemed to be the only one there not overjoyed to be part of the historical moment.

Clinton arrived forty-six minutes late, wowed the crowd, then hung around to sign autographs from a long line of giddy fans. It occurred to me as I started for my car that I was missing a big opportunity. A few years before, I'd traveled with a journalist who'd recently attended a private party in New York at which Clinton was also a guest. Months after the encounter, she was still nearly breathless describing his charisma and flirtatious ways, including his insistence that she save him a dance at an upcoming wedding they both planned to attend. I knew I should experience that famous Clinton charisma for myself, but all I really wanted was to go home, savor the memories of the Mediterranean, finish uploading photos, and pour a glass of wine. But now gone from the port, I was nagged by guilt, by that old familiar question of, What if? He was, after all, President William Jefferson Clinton, and there were all those people, and well, anything could happen, and I wasn't there. This once happened to a colleague who left a fireworks display early only to turn on her TV at home and see an explosion had ripped through the stands. But on that afternoon at the Port of Newport, there were no big surprises, and I remain probably one of a very few people in this town who turned out for Bill Clinton and returned without so much as a handshake.

Meanwhile, the bad news continued. Gas was up to $4.13 a gallon while reimbursement from the *Oregonian* remained stuck at $0.35 a mile. The *Oregonian* announced it was closing a number of bureau offices and looking to cut 10 percent of the workforce. The talk of layoffs and buyouts was constant. Then, as I was attending wildfire training with my Portland colleagues at Camp Rilea, word came that the Newhouse family, owners of the *Oregonian* and numerous other dailies, as well as Condé Naste, had asked for 250 buyouts from the *Star-Ledger* staff in Newark, New Jersey. If they didn't get them, they would sell the paper. With this latest news, there could be no denying the future was bleak. The bad news was tempered ever so slightly by word from Portland that full-timers would no longer have job guarantees, which meant part-timers like myself would no longer be the only ones with targets on their backs. By the end of the summer, the buyouts were on the table. My editor took it, and I moved on to yet another editor. They were gray days, indeed, and about to get even darker.

When I first learned of the murder-suicide that fall in Florence, I almost passed on the story. My editors weren't terribly interested. Murder-suicides, it seemed, were happening all too often. Someone cheats. Someone steals. Someone lies. Someone loses their mind.

But I couldn't seem to let the story go. This was not the usual husband/wife, boyfriend/girlfriend or parent/child. These were two men, both bachelors, both apparently going about their lives in the quiet countryside. What could have caused the end of their lives? Was it a woman? Alcohol? Money? An unwelcome proposition? No, as I was about to find out, it was cats. Two of them.

I set out for the old mill store where Teddy Sellers, sixty-three, had lived, and found a crumbling canary yellow building with orange trim. Neighbors said it rented cheap and attracted "undesirables." On the front porch sat an old refrigerator next to a car seat. A peek through the soiled, cracked windows revealed an interior littered with dirty machine parts, ashtrays, and various odds and ends. It looked not so much like someone's home as a place someone had long ago abandoned, leaving only the old, the odd, the broken behind. It was the kind of place that gave me the creeps just being there, a place that felt like any moment someone was going to jump out of the shadows.

I climbed back in the RAV and went in search of some neighbors who could tell me about the men. Being a rural area, most houses were set back from the road, and as I turned down whatever driveways or side roads I found, I hoped they led to some place friendly. Most of the time, they did—once I got a chance to identify myself and explain what I was up to. But then, after talking with three or four neighbors, I turned down one dirt road and found myself facing a big dead animal, skinned and bloody, hanging by its head from a hook in an open shed. That was the last dirt road for me. I headed home. But I'd learned enough.

Guy Frazier, fifty-seven, lived in a home he'd owned for sixteen years just up the road from the old mill store. He was a gentle soul, with a knack for the guitar and a tendency to keep to himself, neighbors said. Teddy Sellers, on the other hand, was a stranger to most. No one seemed to know much about him. One neighbor described Sellers as an "odd duck." Another said he was a weirdo, and most of the neighbors would not let their children around him. His criminal record showed three misdemeanor counts of assault in the fourth degree.

The men did not get along. Frazier suspected Sellers of snooping around his property when he was gone and accused him of littering on his land. But the dispute that Frazier feared might put him over the edge was the cats. Frazier's cat was not declawed; Sellers's was. When the two cats got into it, as cats will, Sellers said it was unfair fight, so he took matters into his own hands.

When the deputy told me Sellers had declawed Frazier's pet, I admit, I laughed a bit. "So, let me get this straight," I said. "Sellers took Frazier's cat to the vet and had it declawed against Frazier's wishes?" I personally find declawing cats to be cruel and unnecessary, so I could see how Frazier might be pretty pissed off. But murderously?

The deputy wasn't laughing. "No," he said. "He did it himself. He cut off the cat's toes." And then he threw the bloodied cat into Frazier's arms.

That was Halloween morning. The cat fled into the brush and Frazier could not persuade it to come out. He went to a neighbor for help, but after twenty minutes of coaxing the cat, they'd still had no luck. About thirty minutes after his neighbor had last seen Frazier, she heard the gunshot.

It was the mailman who spotted Frazier dragging Sellers's body from the curving Canary Road. Frazier told him that he'd shot him in the head; it was an accident. They thought he was dead and covered him with a sheet of plastic. The mailman left to call for help. Police arrived and found Sellers alive, lying in a pool of blood and vomit. Frazier was gone, believed to be holed up in his house just above the scene.

Meanwhile, in an office in Florence, Frazier's sister listened to talk on the scanner as police gathered on Canary Road. She knew the address, and immediately assumed someone had harmed her brother. He was a passive man, not the kind to hurt another.

Deputies worked through the day to reach Frazier. There was smoke from the chimney and movements around the house. At 2:15 the next morning, they found him hanging in a shed.

Sellers died in the hospital.

Local animal lovers attempted to capture Frazier's cat. I never heard if they were successful.

The story ran a short time after the deaths. And that's when I heard from Sellers's sister. She called our managing editor and wanted a full retraction. It was my job to call her and explain myself. It was not an easy call to make. Her brother was dead. And I had written a story that basically said the guy was a jerk. I explained that I'd asked everyone I could find to tell me about Sellers, and their response was always bad. But I should have known, no matter what the neighbors and acquaintances said about Teddy Sellers, someone, somewhere, loved him. At the time, my brother was still alive. And although being his baby sister by ten years, I was something of a favorite of his; I knew how difficult he could be. I could have probably found plenty of people who thought my brother was a jerk. But I loved him.

And Sellers's sister loved her brother. She told me my karma would catch up with me. I told her about the people I talked to who knew him, about the phone messages I left for people I thought might be family members that were never returned. For three days before I wrote the story, I tried to find someone to paint me a different picture of the man people described as menacing and unpleasant. Obviously, I hadn't found her. She was angry, and I didn't blame her. She was sad. And by the last phone call, when I offered to do a life story on her brother, just as I had for other victims, we were both sobbing. The story never happened, and we never talked again. But I never forgot about that karma comment. That kind of thing stays with you.

I confess there was a time when I rose in the early, dark hours of the morning after Thanksgiving to join in with the rest of the crazed shoppers in scoring Black Friday deals. On November 28, 2008, that day coincided with the first day that commercial crabbers were allowed to set pots— called the pre-soak. They weren't allowed to harvest their catch for another sixty-four hours (changed in the 2014–2015 crab season to seventy-three hours). These rules were designed to make the crab season opening safer by taking away the need to race out to sea.

Early that morning, under a still night sky, as I looked out over the coastline and saw the twinkle of the fleet lights, I had a bad feeling. Maybe it was the crappy weather or the dark or just the knowledge that the crab fishery can be a dangerous one. Or maybe it was because I had recently become friends with Michele Longo Eder, author of *Salt in Our Blood*. Michele lost her son, Ben Eder, to the sea when the F/V *Nesika* capsized in December 2001. Three other crewmen also lost their lives. Michele's husband, Bob, and other son, Dylan, continued to fish. Knowing the family, I think, brought the danger closer to home. Still, I had covered plenty of deaths at sea by then, but never that I could recall on the first day of pre-soak.

We did our shopping at Freddy's with pretty much the rest of the population of Lincoln County, then headed north for the outlets in Lincoln City. Just as we were leaving, I found a message from Todd Anderson. The F/V *Network* had capsized on the Tillamook Bay bar. I called the city desk to see if I should cover it. Technically, I was out of hours, and it was a holiday. But it was a story that needed to be told, and I wasn't inclined to give it away. The editor gave me the okay, so we raced home twenty-odd miles south for my camera, and then seventy-five miles north again to the jetty at Tillamook Bay.

Anderson asked me not to contact the skipper of the boat, Darrin Mobley, the sole survivor, because he deserved his privacy. Anderson was protective like that, and I, grateful for the many phone calls from him alerting me to breaking news, promised to honor his wishes. But he did offer to send two Tillamook deputies to the bar to talk with me. That seemed fair enough. At the jetty, the first person I spoke with led me to his cousin, eyewitness Mark Headley, who was visiting for the holidays from Eugene.

"As he approached the end of the bar, he went into this one huge swell," Headley said. "Its tail stood the boat up. Next thing you know, it was turned around, the lights were off, and it was on the bar."

The two deputies arrived and gave me more details. Missing were George Shaw, fifty-five, of Sequim, Washington, and Tim Leake, forty-four, of Tillamook. Mobley, forty-three, of Bay City, had survived by climbing onto the jetty rocks. The boat was loaded with ninety-seven crab pots, and seas were fourteen to sixteen feet with sharp breaks.

"That's big," Deputy Chuck Reeder said. "That's pretty danged big."

After I finished with the deputies, I walked around talking with others. Someone recalled seeing a survivor in the water waving. The people on the jetty could see him, but the Coast Guard could not. As we spoke, a Coast Guard rescue boat cruised the waters and the helicopter flew overhead.

A woman approached me and tearfully asked, "Do you guys know if Tim Leake was on board?" He was her ex-husband. I took her aside and told her the truth. I left out the part about the man, since disappeared, waving from the water.

SIX

COLD CASES

2009

If I stand in the northwest corner of my living room, the one that looks out to the distant ocean, I can see a spot, just one street away, where the girls were last seen alive—except, of course, by whoever killed them. The house that once occupied the corner is gone, a raggedy old wood garage the only reminder this was once someone's home.

January 2009 marked fourteen years since Jennifer Esson and Kara Leas left Esson's boyfriend's house on a rough stormy night sometime right around 1:00 a.m. It was weeks before their bodies were found, just a couple of miles from where they were last seen.

I had heard stories about other cold cases—at least two of which were frighteningly similar to Esson and Leas—in Lincoln County, and wanted to do a story, but I'd never been able to make it happen. Now, newly elected District Attorney Rob Bovett was in office, and he was not only game for working with me but agreed to put together some detectives and reopen the case. I was finally going to do the story, and I believed it would be a good one.

But after investing days of research and many hours on the telephone, I discovered that my predecessor had already done an anniversary story just four years prior. And I really had nothing new to add. I hated the idea that all the work had been for naught, and I hated even more the idea of not telling a story that might be forgotten if not kept in the public eye. The girls had been murdered; the killer remained unknown. It should not be left to fade away like so much old news. And so I kept looking for something new, something different to warrant another story.

When I found it, it seemed so obvious I couldn't imagine why no one had thought of it before: Was there a serial killer stalking the Oregon coast? Could four of these victims (two other cold cases were too dissimilar, police say) be the work of one person?

Melissa Sanders, seventeen, and Sheila Swanson, nineteen, both of Sweet Home, came to the coast in May of 1992 with the Sanders family for a planned weeklong camping trip at Beverly Beach State Park. But the girls, perhaps bored with small town life on the coast, lasted one day before heading to a phone booth to call for a ride back to town. Six months later, hunters found their bodies twenty miles east of Newport near Eddyville in thick brush about fifty feet from a logging road. The bodies were too badly decomposed for the medical examiner to determine the cause of death.

And then there was Esson and Leas. They'd left the house on NW 56th Street sometime between 12:45 a.m. and 1:30 a.m. on January 28, 1995—a Saturday—telling Esson's boyfriend, Sam Williams, that they were going home. Police initially treated the missing girls as runaways.

Detective Steve Hebner was on duty on February 15 when two loggers walked into the Oregon State Police offices just north of Newport to report they'd found a body about a mile north in the brush above Moolack Beach. Hebner accompanied the loggers to a spot closer to the site and through binoculars saw a hand and pieces of clothing sticking from the brush. On site, detectives found the girls, bodies stacked one on top of the other. Both had been strangled.

In the span of three years, in a county where violent crime is infrequent, there were two cases, with two victims each, both last seen in the same general area of the coast, both found in heavy brush by logging roads.

Bovett scheduled a meeting for me with about a half dozen detectives, some retired, but volunteering their time, to talk about the cases. They didn't have to give me their time or indulge my many questions, but they did so graciously, understanding, I think, that continued publicity was their best hope. They were also hoping new DNA technology might reveal something that had not shown up before.

"I have been waiting for fourteen years for the technology to do this,"

Hebner said. "We finally have a shot. The difference in technology is the difference of looking at the heavens through an Earth-based telescope and now looking at the heavens through the Hubble Space Telescope. It's night-and-day difference."

I posed my theory. Could this be the work of a serial killer?

"Every one of us has wondered exactly that same thing," Hebner, now retired, told me. "If we are lucky enough to find who is responsible for Esson and Leas, I am not going to be at all surprised to find that person is responsible for the others. I cannot drive past Moolack Beach . . . I still see things in my head," he said. "I am not an emotional guy, but I have shed tears about this."

(Note: I would learn nearly ten years later that my hunch was right. Sort of. In 2018, a five-part series that ran in the *Oregonian*, Ghosts of Highway 20, revealed that Lincoln County detectives had tied the deaths of Sanders and Swanson to state highway worker John Ackroyd, who had been imprisoned since 1994—one year before Esson and Leas were murdered. He was charged with the murder of Kaye Turner, who disappeared while running in central Oregon, and of his stepdaughter, Rachanda Pickle.)

My story on the missing teens ran on A1, January 25. My work on the story was done, but the story wasn't done with me.

I've always been pretty sure of my ability to take care of myself. Tough, some people would say. At fourteen, I made weekly trips alone to Philadelphia to attend John Robert Powers modeling school; at eighteen, I moved to Anchorage, at the time, a small city of strip joints, pawn shops, escort services, and all the cocaine and pot you could buy. I had to be street smart and usually I was.

But after my work on the cold cases, I existed in a state of constant fear. I was afraid to be alone in my home. I was afraid to go into the garage. When Chan got up and left for work, I got up and checked the locks. Sometimes I'd find myself standing in the northwest corner staring across the houses and yards to the corner on 56th Street. The house the girls had visited was gone. The girls were gone. I became haunted by the story and went over and over the details—the detectives' report that the girls had struggled hard, put up a hell of a good fight, very nearly got away. Shoelaces bound one of their hands. And the curious comment Leas made to Esson's boyfriend Sam Williams. That night, as they were leaving, Leas told Williams if he didn't hear from her in an hour and a half to call the police.

I can think of only two reasons a teenaged girl would say such a thing—they were young and it was 1:00 a.m. on a stormy night. Highway 101 in January in the wee hours of the morning is a lonely, dark, even foreboding place. Maybe she was being dramatic the way a teen girl can be. Or maybe they'd made plans to meet someone—the kind of date any teen girl knows is risky as hell, but also the kind of date many teen girls can't resist for its promise of adventure, the hint of a visit to the dark—but not too dark—side.

I had been such a teen, hitchhiking when I needed to get somewhere, dating men with less than stellar pasts. I'd been sexually assaulted, smacked around a bit, and more than once talked my way out of what was promising to turn ugly. Once the man I'd left an Anchorage bar with asked, "You know I could kill you, don't you?"

But here I am. Esson and Leas didn't get to talk their way out of it.

Through it all, I got to know Barb Tucker, the tearful woman who eyed me so skeptically that day in Fred Meyer when I introduced myself. Tucker is married to Esson's half-brother, Rocky Tucker. Often, when I shopped at Fred Meyer, I'd stop and talk to her, always hoping for some hint of a break. But for years there were none, and Barb Tucker was losing hope. I understood why. I had hoped this renewed interest with my story might bring something new to light, but in the end, even all that new technology was not enough.

As it turned out, the story didn't end there. Three years would pass before the day when I just happened to be sitting in the Fred Meyer parking lot and found Rob Bovett's name on my cell phone. It was one of those conversations that was purely off the record, but it would turn out to be one of the biggest breaking stories of my career.

Meanwhile, the bad news for journalists just kept coming. A month or so earlier, Mary, my old editor from the *Rocky*, called to tell me Scripps had put the paper on the market. If it didn't sell by mid-January, they would close it. "It is like a bomb hit the newsroom," she said. Nobody believed the paper would sell. The days of two-newspaper towns were long gone, and there were other newspapers already on the market.

The *Seattle Post Intelligencer* was also up for sale and would stop publishing the print edition if there was no buyer. At about the same time, the *Denver Post* ran a story that said it would be the sole Denver newspaper as of March 1. Scripps denied it. On Friday the 13th, I got a heads up from my editors that cuts were coming at the *Oregonian*, and I was vulnerable. It was getting old. Just when we thought we were stabilizing there'd be word of more buyouts, layoffs, furloughs. But work went on. Meanwhile, I had developed problems with my right shoulder, which was growing ever more painful. A grocery store courtesy clerk named Steve, retired from the Coast Guard and now working at Safeway, diagnosed it as a torn rotator cuff. I was hoping he was wrong, but suspected he was right. In any case, once I alerted Steve to my pain, I never carried a single grocery bag.

Late February, I was in a Tillamook hotel room waiting to go on Oregon Public Broadcasting's *Think Out Loud*. The topic was Navy warfare training off of the Oregon and Washington coasts. I'd covered the public hearing the night before. The Navy was increasing the number of training operations, and people worried about the environmental impacts on marine life. They were also upset about the lack of notice and public input. On the other side of the table were parents of soldiers who wanted their children to get proper training.

Minutes before show time, someone sent me a link to a video. The *Denver Post* had been telling the truth. One hundred and forty-nine years, three hundred and eleven days after the first edition hit the streets, the *Rocky Mountain News* was coming to an end. I watched the video, recorded during the *Rocky*'s final days, in tears. Then I dried my eyes to do the radio show. But they didn't stay dry long.

The *Rocky* was my first major metro daily. I was hired for a new Sunday section, Home Front, and as badly as I wanted the job, I was also scared to death. There were some seriously talented writers at the *Rocky*, writers who'd studied at the big J-schools, writers who won prizes and vied for the Pulitzer. My editor, Mary, who I would come

Press car plate.

to think of as my surrogate big sister, assigned fellow reporter James Meadow to be my newsroom buddy. He promptly put the notion to rest, explaining he didn't do the buddy thing, especially not the tour of the building. But if I needed anything to let him know. I spent those first few months certain someone was going to out me for the fraud I feared I was, and the gig would be up. I worked at my stories for hours on end, going in early in the morning before most anyone else got to work and the newsroom was still quiet. I studied writers like James for clues to how they did what they did so well. And mostly I just put my head down and charged.

My beat was home décor—or more accurately—writing about very rich people's homes: homes with indoor bowling alleys and outdoor heated pools by mountain resort ski runs, old Denver mansions with massive fireplaces in the kitchen and carriage houses in the back. Soon, I had my own column—also about homes, though the concept could be stretched a lot of different ways.

I wrote about the Parade of Homes and the Denver Jr. Symphony's Show House, always grinning just a little to myself at the irony—me, the daughter of a mother who probably could not have defined interior design—hanging with the well-heeled. Sometimes, though, I hated the beat. The snootiness, the easy money, the egos, the blatant appeal from designers and design shops for stories in the paper even though they were above advertising in our tabloid-sized *Rocky*, opting instead for the tony home magazines.

The *Rocky*'s size made it both beloved and belittled. Some associated it with the tabloids like the *National Enquirer* or worse. Once, as we sat at lunch with an architect we featured often, he admitted that his problem with the *Rocky* was that people thought of it as the newspaper for the working class. I considered stabbing him with my fork. I admit I was somewhat oblivious to the huge class divide in this country until I worked that gig. Oh, I knew there were the moneyed and the not. I just didn't quite get that if you were, say, a power lineman, you inhabited a lower rung on the ladder than, oh, an attorney—even if you did make more money.

Sometimes I got drafted to write for other editors in the feature sections. Once, I wrote about installing a sprinkler system, another time about a survival race, and once, a story about the Brazilian martial art capoeira. When news of the Columbine massacre broke, I was drafted to write a description of the school for the afternoon extra edition. I'd never seen the school and to this day, never have. Instead, on that afternoon as we watched the story breaking live on the newsroom TVs, I called sources my colleagues shared with me—a coach, a former teacher, a neighbor—and let them describe the school.

The Columbine shooting remains the darkest memory from my days in the Denver newsroom, but there are plenty of other stories that stay with me, as well, though not necessarily for their newsworthiness. Few were more eye-opening than the debutante ball I was assigned to cover one spring. Me and the debs. An odder pairing I can hardly imagine, but there we were. My assignment was to choose one young woman to follow throughout the season while she learned all the proper form and function before the big night. I attended a fashion show and an early primer on curtseying, trying to figure which girl would make the best story. Soon, I became very popular with all the debs' mothers, particularly a woman we'll just call Buffy, who was married to a very rich and very powerful man and was, by all accounts, a bitch beyond compare. Buffy made a big play at being my friend, even hinting at a possible distant familial connection, but of course, what Buffy really wanted was for me to choose her daughter to follow and write about.

I did not. Instead I chose Martha, a young woman fairly new to town, recently relocated from Georgia with a lovely family and all that Southern grace and manners. I followed her to the bridal boutique as she chose her dress from a storeroom of ivory and white taffeta and lace, some carrying price tags of $10,000 (and this was pre-2000). And I began to learn about the makings of a debutante, about waltzing, drinking tea, posture, and speech, and all the kinds of things they don't teach you in public schools. I learned the four-point curtsey, in which the deb puts her left leg behind her right, bends to receive her tiara, then straightens and brings her feet back together. Not nearly so difficult as the curtsey taught back East, where the debs must touch their nose to the floor. "Can you imagine that?" Jaylene Smith, ball cochairwoman, asked. "We thought that was too hard, and besides not very ladylike. If your nose is down on the floor, then your butt has got to be up in the air."

The story was not without its detractors, for obvious reasons. The entry fee alone was $1,500, and while the debutante organizers insisted it was good grades, leadership, impeccable manners, and community involvement that earned the girls an invite, I doubt I could have found one young lady whose family were not members of one country club or another. And the debs, of course, loved the whole fairy princess experience.

"It was always something I knew I'd do," Martha told me. She remembered seeing pictures of her mother in full deb finery. "Every little girl's dream is to be crowned . . . to be a star for a night."

Truthfully, it was kind of fun—in an ironic, thank-God-this-is-a-one-time-thing kind of way.

On the eve of the ball, we sat outside the country club on rows of folding chairs as the skies turned dark and the air grew moist, and everyone prayed it would not rain. It never did, the organizer insisted, as if to suggest that even the elements knew better than to rain on the debutantes' parade. Someone handed out Hefty leaf bags (the rich really are no different from the rest of us when it comes to the prospect of looking like drowned rats) and soon the first drops fell. The debs were protected beneath a roof, but the rest of us had to suffer. They hurried through the ceremony, and finally we all moved inside to dry out. I was talking to Martha's mother. Suddenly, there was a hand on my shoulder, followed by a shove.

"You're in my kitchen now," Buffy hissed. (My writing mentor told me never to write that word, but I swear that's exactly what she did.) My work finished, I left a short time later, and that was the end of my inclusion in the world of debutantes and their mothers. Or almost the end, anyway.

My story ran a few days later. I was proud of it, proud of having figured out how to write about a world as foreign to me as Mar-a-Lago. The morning it ran, I couldn't resist calling the deb's mother. Polite as ever, but in a voice worried and small, she reported she had been unable to leave her bed after seeing I'd quoted her on the exorbitant cost of the ball gowns. Apparently, the country club set would not be quite so welcoming in the coming days.

Nor was my own newsroom. I soon learned my story was the subject of a morning radio show, ridiculed and rejected as elitist bullshit, and I was presumed one of the country club set, ridiculously out of touch with reality. Even some of my colleagues joined in. For a few short hours that day, I belonged nowhere, not with the working-class journalists I called friends, and certainly not with the debutante crowd. It didn't last long, but it hurt.

Over time at the *Rocky*, I grew surer, though I never stopped studying the writers I admired. James and I were friends by then. We joked about judging the Miss America pageant, something we both did sitting before the TV with our pens and yellow legal pads. And we shared vegetarian recipes. He had had some health scares involving his heart and was changing his eating habits. I hadn't eaten meat, poultry, or seafood for about five years by then. I brought him my favorite vegetarian cookbooks and sought out others from the library. Soon, he was bringing me recipes, too.

When I returned to visit in 2007, James was the one person I meant to see when I visited the newsroom. I saw him cross the room to his desk and thought he was my next stop. But then there was someone else to catch up with, and then someone else, and I had left before I realized I'd never made it to his desk.

Less than two weeks after the *Rocky* closed, I was in Mexico on the beach. I saw someone had tried several times to reach me on my cell. Just before we left, the *Oregonian* had announced more layoffs were imminent, but they would ask for volunteers first.

So there I was with hordes of bikinied, drunk spring breakers sipping and sunning. And there was reality in the form of a caller I didn't recognize. The calls began at 9:00 a.m., the same time many of my editors arrived at work. I hit the call back button and listened to it ring as I watched Chan rip along the sea before me on a jet ski. I didn't know it at the time, but he was actually rescuing two guys who'd crashed their ski and were thrashing in the water shouting for help.

"Hello," a woman answered.

"Hey, this is Lori; you were trying to reach me."

"Oh Lori," she said. "It's Mary . . . Is this a good time?"

I laughed. "Of course." I was always happy to hear from Mary.

"Lori," she said. "I'm sorry to have to tell you this. James Meadow died."

The next month, the *Seattle Post-Intelligencer* published its last print edition, while I waited for the news of my fate. First, it looked like I'd be gone, then not, then surely the next round of layoffs and then maybe not then, either. In the end, twenty-four employees were laid off. Those who survived were rewarded with a 10 percent pay cut. They canceled the annual awards luncheon and warned of more layoffs to come. While numerous readers reached out to me, many others commented that we journalists—often we fucking liberal journalists or some version thereof—deserved this. It was the same when the *Rocky* closed. I should not have been surprised, but the pain was fresh every time.

How did once-thriving daily newspapers, thick with ads and inserts, just go away? It's pretty straightforward, John Temple, my editor at the *Rocky* and, later, managing editor at the *Washington Post* and *Honolulu Civil Beat*, told me.

"Realistically, America's changed," Temple said. "People stopped working in factories. That led to the decline of the afternoon newspaper. In the contemporary world, it really stems from the Internet. Probably the first big blow to the newspaper industry was Craigslist and the fact that classifieds, which were a very important component to the revenue of newspapers, became free. It completely undermined the news classified business. Most lucrative were always the job listings, known as career classifieds. Those were highly profitable ads. That was one of the first blows, and then it really continued from there.

"Effectively, the Internet has a better vehicle for targeting advertisers to consumers than newspapers offered. It is an industry in collapse. It has not been able to make the transition to digital."

But in 2009, there were still plenty of people who appreciated the power of the press and understood how it could (sometimes) work for them. Which was how I found myself writing about Karen Noyes and the bears. Noyes wanted her story of grave injustice known, and the farther and wider the better.

Usually, I would agree with the desire to share such a story. Whenever there is an injustice, an abuse of power, the little guy getting trounced by the bigger one, there is no better way to right that wrong than to splash that story in the boldest possible hues across every media outlet on the planet: newspapers, TV, radio, and now, of course, Twitter, Facebook, and all the other social media. The one time this is definitely not the route to take is when you, in fact, have courted disaster all on your own. And by interacting with animals that could have easily killed her, Noyes clearly had.

Noyes had been charged with nine counts of animal harassment and human endangerment. Two weeks before she was due in court, she called my editor with her tale. And since Noyes lives in Yachats, a coastal town, my editor called me. And so began the story of the woman people referred to as the Bear Lady.

On the afternoon I called her, she began our conversation by proclaiming, "I feed bears. It's not illegal." Just then, there were about half a dozen bears in her Yachats back yard, she said. Once she'd counted twenty-five, a personal record. "The biggest one sitting there right now is six hundred pounds. The males get big. They bring their babies.' As someone noted, cubs don't usually follow the males, but to Noyes's thinking, it seemed they did.

I know a few black bear stories myself. Most of my bear stories are from Alaska and involve grizzlies. In Alaska, if you have a bear story, and it's just a little old black bear, generally, you can't expect your audience to be too impressed. But a hungry bear is a hungry bear regardless of its kind.

I thought Noyes should know that, so I told her my bear story. It happened in July 1992. I was visiting Alaska at the time. A couple was vacationing in their cabin about 160 miles northeast of Anchorage when a black bear came through the cabin window. The husband scared it off with a couple of shots from a .22, then went for help. He sent his wife to wait for him on the cabin roof, figuring she'd be safe. The bear climbed a spruce tree to the roof. When he returned with help, his wife was on the ground dead, and the bear was eating her.

Noyes listened, or at least seemed to, but when I finished, she was right back on track.

"When I get home, they are usually in the yard," she explained. "I wait until I see them. I put the food out then. Black sunflower seeds. They are perfectly safe. Timid and shy. They are really sweet."

She told me she'd started feeding animals in 1992 after her husband of eleven years died when his pickup truck struck a tree and went over a cliff. That came just a year after her daughter died of health problems after years of drug abuse.

That she was due in court on nine different charges was all Oregon Department of Fish and Wildlife agent Tami Wagner's fault, Noyes said. It had all been a misunderstanding. The summer before, one of the bears had broken Noyes's window. He was not being malicious, Noyes said. On the contrary, he was actually knocking on the garage door, but accidentally got the window. She called Fish and Wildlife to ask some questions,

Karen Noyes believed feeding the local bears was harmless.

and Wagner offered to send someone to help her. That someone came in January when it was raining, and Noyes's beau had just moved out, and she was feeling lonely. I'm sure she was. In January on the Oregon coast, everyone is feeling lonely. She invited the agent in. He saw the picture of her feeding the bears and took it with him. She was due in court in about two weeks. Bear expert Lynn Rogers, a biologist featured on Animal Planet TV's *The Man Who Walks with Bears*, was the star witness scheduled to testify on her behalf.

I sat behind Noyes on that day in May as her trial got under way. She was a slight woman with vivid hair the color of fire, likeable enough and wanting to be liked. When the judge called for a recess, and her attorney walked off, I introduced myself. She was happy to see me, eager to help. I asked if she had photos. She looked around, then seeing no one of import in the courtroom, slipped open her lawyer's file, and pulled a colorful shot of her feeding, by hand, a cluster of grapes to a fairly good-sized black bear.

It was just plain crazy. But while the idea of this tiny sixty-one-year-old woman fearlessly feeding these bears in her backyard was good for a few grins, when the witnesses started taking the stand to explain how those same bears had impacted their lives, it was anything but funny. One neighbor wouldn't close the barn doors for fear a bear would get in and the horses would have no way out. Another lost more than sixty heritage turkeys to the bears. Still another awoke to a commotion she thought was a raccoon. She climbed out of bed to find a black bear coming through the dog door. Later, it became one of four bears shot dead in a four-week period the previous summer.

That morning, when court again recessed, I hoped to get an interview with Noyes, but she'd disappeared in the crowd. Then I saw her at the last moment headed for the ladies' room. The only other reporter covering the trial was Larry Coonrod, a staff writer at the *Newport News-Times*. He watched me follow her in, shaking his head. Life really wasn't fair. I asked Noyes about the testimony we'd just heard, but she insisted it had nothing to do with her feeding the bears. Rather, as Rogers would testify, Noyes believed that by feeding the bears she was reducing the problem, eliminating their need to search out food elsewhere.

Later that day, I caught up with Tami Wagner, who I'd previously worked with on a couple of other wildlife stories. We talked about the case. Wagner shared her thoughts on the psychology behind the behavior of people who anthropomorphize wild animals. And then moments later, she disappeared. When I saw her again, she seemed to want to avoid me. Later, I approached her, and she explained that she'd caught hell from her supervisor for saying such things to a reporter, which could get the agency sued. I tried to assure her that I wouldn't print any of it, but she wouldn't stick around long enough to hear even that.

Back in my office, I called and left a message to make sure she knew she had nothing to worry about. I was always glad I made that call.

In the end, Noyes was found guilty of one count of chasing and harassing wildlife, and given a sentence that shocked the courtroom. Lincoln County Circuit Judge Thomas Branford spoke for more than thirty minutes before delivering his sentence. She would get probation and fines, but most importantly she was banned from her home for three years. He likened the special condition to requiring a drunk driver to stay out of bars.

"I find your letter to the newspaper stunning," Branford said, referring to Noyes's missive in the local newspaper. "You have twisted this story to the point of being unrecognizable to anything close to reality. I couldn't agree more with the jury's verdict."

In explaining the $5,000 fine to be paid at $150 a month, Branford said by her own tally, Noyes had reported spending $100,000 in the past five years feeding the bears.

"At $100,000 over five years, that's $20,000 a year, $1,066 a month, or $50 a day to feed the bears," Branford said. "If you stop feeding the bears, it will save you $15,000 a year. For you, this is a cheap fine."

The next day, Noyes called me.

"I don't know why I am here if I can't feed the wildlife," she said.

Her voice was flat. But it wasn't until I hung up that I wondered exactly what she'd meant. Was she thinking about ending her life? I rang her back, but now the phone was busy. I called my editor, and we discussed if I should drive to her house and make sure she was okay, but Noyes lived at least forty-five minutes away, and other than the name of the road, I had no real idea where.

I hung up with my editor and dialed Noyes again. This time, she answered. I asked if she was okay. She said she was. I told her things would get better, and offered a few other kind words. When I hung up, I called my editor again.

"You know," I said. "Days like this, I just want to bleach my hair blond and take up bartending."

For as long as I'd been on the job, I'd heard about the unsolved cold case of a young teenaged girl found dead in 2000. Sometimes, I'd get an email from someone hoping I'd take up the case or I'd see a blurb in the local Coos Bay paper. But I'd never been able to make time for it. Then came a call from a woman doing volunteer public relations for the dead girl's mother. They desperately wanted me to do the story, and I agreed it was time.

It had been nine and a half years since Leah Freeman went missing from a Coquille street on a June evening in 2000. She was fifteen years old. One shoe was found by the local cemetery later that night; the second was found on a dirt road far out of town. Five weeks later, searchers found her body.

The case was cold. Police had questioned and questioned again Freeman's boyfriend, Nick McGuffin. They offered Brent Bartley, who was with McGuffin that night, immunity to testify against his friend, but Bartley said no. I heard the suspicions, the reasons behind them, but it never added up to me. McGuffin had spent the better part of the night looking for Freeman, who'd left her friend's home shortly before 9:00 p.m. and was last seen striding up Central Avenue about fifteen minutes later. Somehow I couldn't see an eighteen-year-old having the presence of mind to kill his girlfriend, ditch her body, clean himself up, and then spend hours running around town, asking people if they'd seen her. But it seemed police had not seriously considered any other subject.

I drove to Coquille to meet Leah's mother, who was determined that her daughter not be forgotten, that her killer be caught and brought to justice. I drove out to the place where they found her body, down a dark, dense, overgrown embankment on a lonely back road with no cell coverage. It didn't take long for this writer's imagination to kick into overdrive, and by the time I got back into sunlight and cell coverage, I was trembling.

The story ran on November 5. One week later, I got word that a woman who lived close to the area where Freeman's body was found was now also missing and police feared the ending would not be good. Jayme Sue Austin had failed to show up at her job. Her mother, Cindy Gisholt, had talked to her earlier that day when Austin called to ask to use her shower. At home, she found her daughter's car window open, the inside soaked from a recent rain. In the house, the bathroom rug was wet and folded on the counter. The floor had been newly vacuumed and inside the vacuum, Gisholt found shells from the pukka necklace Austin always wore.

Austin's disappearance so close to my story and her home's proximity to where Freeman's body was dumped felt awfully coincidental to me, but I seemed to be the only one thinking there might be a connection. In the morning, an assistant from Nancy Grace called to ask me to do the TV show via telephone. I agreed, and sent a new mug shot for them to post on the show while I talked. When Grace asked what else I could tell them, I shared the Leah Freeman story. They asked me to call in again the next night. I did the second show from a hotel room, while waiting to fly back to Pennsylvania. But this time Grace built her show around everything I'd told her assistant before we went on the air, and when it came time for Miss Expert here to share the inside scoop, I had nothing more to add.

In the morning, as I walked through PDX, I read that Austin's brother-in-law, Patrick Horath, had confessed and led police to her body buried in a shallow grave. I never did another story on Austin, but years later I would end up with a fairly significant role in a television documentary and a guest appearance in another show about the case.

But the Leah Freeman story wasn't finished. Not long after my story ran, a grand jury indicted Nick McGuffin. Until then, I had made it no secret that I didn't believe he was guilty, and I certainly didn't believe the state had a case against him. It wasn't a bias, but merely my assessment of the facts against him. Aside from him being her boyfriend, there really weren't any. Although there was plenty of rumor. Once, while having my makeup done at Macy's in Portland, the young makeup artist, originally from Coquille, informed me that everyone knew McGuffin had killed Freeman because she was pregnant and he didn't want a child. While they never determined how Freeman died, I can't imagine them overlooking a pregnancy.

A year and a half after the indictment, I showed up for McGuffin's trial at the cavernous old Coos County Courthouse to find that the judge was blocking the media from voir dire—jury selection. Day two, we discovered that the judge was planning to offer only five seats for reporters during the trial and no opportunity to watch it on television remotely—the option other judges usually offer in a case where the courtroom will be packed. He also would not allow anyone to stand in the courtroom. I called the newsroom and explained what was going on. Moments later, an editor called me back to say the judge is not allowed to bar the media from voir dire.

"We may need you to respectfully request a delay in the trial so our attorney can file a motion," she said.

The prospect of doing so completely unnerved me. I was supposed to stand up in front of a packed courtroom and tell the judge he had to stop? I shared the news with my fellow reporters, who were also fed up with the proceedings. They thought it was a good idea and wondered if the *Oregonian* would entertain the notion of letting their newspapers sign on to the proposed lawsuit. I wasn't even sure any of us were going to get inside the courtroom. As it turned out, the editors declined to shell out money to take on a backwater judge, and finally, as the trial was set to begin, a deputy appeared in the hallway to announce there would be ten seats set aside.

But that was the only improvement. During a recess I attempted to ask the deputy district attorney a question, only to have the Coos County District Attorney bite my head off in front of the entire courtroom. It ranked then and still does as one of the most embarrassing public moments of my career.

Because it was never certain we'd have seats once we left, lunch was a pack of crackers and a soda consumed while standing outside the courtroom by the metal detector so I could be sure of getting back in.

That afternoon I filed my story on the opening arguments and headed home, then discovered—too late—that I'd spelled the deputy DA's name wrong. Ten days later, I was back for the closing arguments. The case went to the jury at 3:00 p.m., and I settled in to wait, only to get a message from the defense attorney that the judge had sent the jurors home with instructions to return at 8:45 a.m. I filed a story from my hotel room, then learned the next morning I had misspelled the defense attorney's name. I couldn't seem to get anything right, and all I wanted was to go home.

Two hours after they were seated, the jury came in with its verdict. Once again, we gathered in the courtroom. It always seems to take forever from the time the judge gets the slip of paper from the jury foreman until he reads it. It must seem doubly so for the defendant.

The judge cleared his throat and read. Not guilty of murder. Then, the judge queried the jury on the alternate charge of manslaughter.

"Guilty," the foreman said.

McGuffin gasped and jumped from his chair as if he'd literally been shocked. He was sentenced to ten years. (His appeal was denied in 2013.) I still didn't believe he was guilty. Rather, I agreed with a comment posted on my story. Coquille needed someone to pay and McGuffin was the only option. As one Portland attorney said to me on hearing the case, "Not only did the DA fail to prove McGuffin killed her, he didn't even prove she was murdered."

While working on this memoir, I wrote McGuffin in prison and asked if he would talk about what he thought had happened to Freeman. I also mentioned that I'd always believed he was innocent. He wrote back, thanking me for contacting him, but said he couldn't discuss the case as he was in the first stage of Post-Conviction Relief—a post-trial procedure that allows a defendant to bring more evidence or raise issues after he or she has been convicted. "I continue to fight to prove my innocence and one day to possibly be able to solve this, and find the true person or people responsible," he wrote. At the time he still had roughly four years left of his sentence.

Then, in December 2019, I learned that McGuffin's conviction had been overturned and he had been granted a new trial. Attorneys with the Forensic Justice Project had discovered that DNA from an unidentified male had been found on Freeman's shoe, but that information, which the prosecution knew of, had not been revealed to the jury during his original trial. It was at Coos County DA Paul Frasier's discretion to retry McGuffin, which he declined to do. Because of his decision, today McGuffin has a clean record. He served all but eight months of his ten-year sentence.

I was gaining a reputation for being in the "right" place at the "right" time.

Of course, often as not that meant happening onto something that was not particularly good news. So it was that August morning as I set out in the fog for a run on the beach. It was the kind of fog that inspired someone to one day long ago craft the simile "thick as pea soup." I generally ran from Agate Beach to Nye Beach and back. For me, a very slow, not particularly natural runner, it took about thirty minutes. I was perhaps three-quarters of the way there when I saw a mass I didn't recognize.

I don't remember there being a rock there, I thought. That was about the same time I realized I was much farther out on the beach than normal. It was a low, low tide, and with the fog obscuring my view, I had drifted west. I would have been running in deep surf if the tide had not been so low. I started to angle back toward shore, growing closer to the unfamiliar mass. A few minutes later, I saw that it was not a rock or part of the headlands, but a boat. A big boat. As I got nearer, I could see cars and trucks on the beach. A boat had run aground. I had no pad, pen, or camera, and my cell was back in the parking lot in my car. So I turned around and started running as hard as I could run. Which was far from impressive. It took, of course, forever. By the time I got to the RAV, my heels were bloody from the sand that had filled my running shoes and rubbed them raw. (So tore up were my feet that, for weeks after, I would have no choice but to run barefoot.) Breathlessly, I called the city desk.

Could we post something right away?

No, I said. I don't even know what kind of boat it is. If it was intact. Or anything about it. Given the fog and visibility, there was even a slim chance I was mistaken. I raced home, threw on clothing that didn't reek of sweat, grabbed my camera, pad and pen, and hurried back to Nye Beach.

There I met Philip Wormington, one of the two men who had been on board. I introduced myself as always, and we began chatting. He was in good spirits as he watched the efforts of the Coast Guard and others to secure the fifty-four-foot boat and figure out how best to get it off of the beach without damaging the environment. He told me about waking in his bunk to the sound of a loud bang and knowing they were in trouble. The skipper, Travis Vitale, twenty-five, of Eureka, California, had fallen asleep, and the fishing vessel, newly renamed the *Lori Ann* (formerly the *Little Linda*) had beached itself. Neither of the crewmembers had been hurt, and now the biggest concern was finding buyers for the five tons of tuna they'd caught in the past eleven days, and making sure the eighteen hundred gallons of fuel was contained.

The F/V Little Linda *grounded on Nye Beach.*

As Wormington told me his tale, I was astonished to see children playing in the water by the boat. They laughed as they raced in the surf, and their parents watched smiling at the kids' easy fun. I couldn't help thinking it was a little like playing Russian roulette with a seventy-ton gun. One big wave, one bounce of the boat, and it would be on top of them. I wasn't the only one watching gape-mouthed, but the kids played on, the authorities apparently too busy with their investigation to intervene.

Later, after he'd told me his story, Wormington turned to me. "Who are you again?" he asked. Back home, the story posted and the comments began, including one reader who wrote, "Of course the boat ran aground. Everyone knows it is bad luck to rename a boat."

It had been a dark summer, and I needed something light, so when I got a call from the Oregon Coast Aquarium to see if I might be interested in a story on "flipper art" and the sea lions that created it, I said yes. Over the years, I'd written about the critters at the aquarium many, many times, and would continue to do so in the years ahead, but few stories stick with me like that of Lea.

It all started with mammologist Jen DeGroot, who was looking for a way to keep the sea lions from growing bored. DeGroot had once worked at an aquarium that did penguin foot prints by having the penguins walk on the canvas, and at another that taught the sea lions to paint holding a brush. DeGroot decided she would teach Lea and Max to "paint" with their flippers. Staff sponged paint onto the front flippers, then pressed canvas to the flipper to create the art. As they worked, they rewarded the sea lions with many, many, many snacks of herring. As Lea finished her task, DeGroot asked if I'd like to experience a sea lion kiss. It never occurred to me to say no. I mean, how often does that opportunity arise? She brought Lea close to me, gave the command, and Lea pressed her little mouth to mine. Just as Cindy Hanson, public relations coordinator, snapped a picture of our kiss, Lea belched, and I inhaled the stink of countless little fishes, the reek of which, I swear, I can still smell to this day.

Summer turned to fall, and we seemed to be getting a reprieve from the more recent winters' storms. Then one Saturday morning, I heard about a tornado striking Lincoln City the night before. It would turn out to be one

A first kiss. Photo by Cindy Steensland (née Hanson).

of those times when being on site at the time of breaking news was not so smart. Right place, wrong time.

The skies were a little gray that morning in Newport, but it wasn't even raining so I assumed the bad weather had passed. Chan and I loaded our rescue pups Mugs and Doozi into the RAV, and the four of us headed up north for a look. We don't get tornados around here. We rarely even get a real thunderstorm, so I figured this deserved a story.

The skies darkened somewhat as we drove, but nothing worrisome. Then we hit Lincoln City, about twenty miles north, and suddenly it was black, pouring rain, hailing, lightning. I wasn't worried about myself. I was worried about the dogs. We'd lost our lab mix Linus to uncontrollable seizures just two months before, and the loss was still so fresh I dissolved in tears at least once a day. When we got to the neighborhood where the tornado had hit, I climbed out to knock on doors.

"If anything happens, just get yourself and the dogs to safety," I told Chan. "I can take care of myself." Which was a show of false bravado if there ever was one.

In central Pennsylvania where I grew up, violent thunderstorms are the norm. And yes, you can add that to another one of those things that scare me—big thunder boomers. I don't mind the nice, mellow rumbling ones, but when it starts to crack and flash, I generally hide out in a dark room, preferably where there are no windows. I never experienced a tornado firsthand, but early in my career got as close as I ever want to.

In 1989, I was working at my first real newspaper job in New Britain, Connecticut. On that afternoon I had driven to visit a family with an autistic son for a story about the difficulty of getting a good education for him. As we talked, a storm blew through outside, but it had mostly died down by the time I left. The first sign that something wasn't right came from the radio when I heard the announcer instruct people to go to an elementary school if they needed shelter or were missing family members. At our apartment in Rocky Hill, I found my husband packing his tramp bag—a big orange bag linemen carry their tools in—and lacing his tall leather boots.

"I don't think I'll be home for a while," he said. "Probably at least a few days. Maybe longer." He was still a young journeyman and hadn't worked a lot of big storms yet, so we really didn't know what to expect. But I worried. I always would.

And I still didn't know for sure what had happened. Only that a storm, possibly a tornado, had struck Hamden, about twenty-five miles south of us. It was just beyond our newspaper's circulation area, but two days later when I told the managing editor that my husband was working it, he sent me and a photographer south.

To this day, I've never seen devastation like it—homes crushed, cars turned upside down, powerlines down. One vivid memory was an old Cadillac stuck in the side of a house on the second floor. Miraculously, only one person was killed.

It was to be the page one centerpiece. My first. I told my editor all about what I had seen and then sat to write. Hours later, he read my story, then harrumphed and said, "Why can't reporters write the way they talk?" I took a second shot. This time I wrote in the present tense, trying to write it as I had described to him. It not only worked; it was the best thing I'd written to that day.

That afternoon when the paper came out, I grabbed a copy to read my front-page story. Two paragraphs in, my heart sank. One of the city desk editors had inserted a couple of lines—in past tense. The best thing I had written in my young career, and it was ruined.

Chan worked for five days straight. One afternoon, he called to tell me to meet him that evening at an upscale restaurant in New Haven. As I waited for the guys in the lobby, I overheard the manager instruct his staff, "We've got a group of linemen coming in; they're not going to be dressed to code, and we're not going to say a word. They've been out working in the storm all week, and this is how we are thanking them."

The guys arrived a short time later. We took up several tables, but Chan and I barely got to talk. He seemed to be in a fog, and when the waitress came for his order and asked did he want corn or salad with his meal, he made her repeat it three times. It was as if he'd never heard of either, and his brain just couldn't process it. It was scary to watch. That evening, he called to say it was over. He was coming home. Six weeks later, a lineman was killed working a storm nearby.

So now here I was working a tornado story on the Oregon coast. I began walking around the neighborhood, shooting pictures of the damage. Houses and cars were damaged over a span of about three blocks. Trees and powerlines were down. But compared to what I'd witnessed in Connecticut, it was mild. Still, that dark sky didn't make it any less scary, and too late, I realized I'd left my cell in the RAV. I knocked on the door of the waterfront house opposite one that lost its roof. The couple, vacationers, welcomed me inside, then explained how the night before they had stood at the plate glass doors watching the tornado grow from a water spout. They had no idea what they were seeing, except that it was fascinating to watch. They described how the streetlights had lit up the swirling water, illuminating it against the dark ocean and blackened night sky. Then the spout grew even bigger and began to move toward them. Only then did it occur to them to hit the floor.

Outside, I found Chan cruising worriedly up the street, searching for some sign of me. By then, the storm had passed, the skies lightened, and our Oregon coast once again felt safe.

SEVEN

THE STARS

2010

It was the first dark story in a year destined for darkness. I learned about the tragedy not long after we'd celebrated the beginning of 2010, in a motel room two hours from home. It was our first year celebrating New Year's Eve at the beachfront, dog-friendly motel in Manzanita. We'd celebrated the holiday in a lot of memorable places: twice in Times Square; once at the top of the Space Needle (the same year a drunk driver crashed into a crowd of people); and one year, we rode the Alaska Railroad train to Whittier, a tiny town accessible at the time only by boat or train. Lately, our celebrations tended to be quiet, just us and the dogs.

That night in Manzanita, we heard the party burst from the pub just moments before midnight. I got outside in time to see the crowd parading down Laneda Avenue. When they reached me at the beach, I handed out horns, clinked my champagne glass with dozens of strangers, and joined in a round of "Auld Lang Syne."

Back inside the motel, I took one last look at my laptop before going to bed and saw a news alert about an armed man in the parking lot of the Lincoln County Courthouse. It was too late to do anything about it then, but I knew the phone would be ringing in the morning.

The call came from the city desk just after I'd gotten rolled in the Pacific during my first—and probably last—Polar Bear Plunge. But I discovered my laptop had picked up a virus, rendering it unusable and giving me a legit excuse to pass up the assignment on a holiday. My colleague ended up writing the brief, the only story that would run in the *Oregonian*. And that was too bad.

It started out as a planned murder-suicide, a seemingly inescapable end for two desperate people living out their lives in a manufactured home just a few miles from my own. In the end, it was more sad than sinister, as much an indictment of our society as the man who wielded the gun.

It seemed there was more to the story that warranted sharing, and so I attempted to write about Daniel Gopshes, sixty, and his wife, Chancey Ann, eighty-six, several times. But every time I dug in, something more important called me away, and in the end I let it go. But it's always stayed with me.

And it's always felt wrong.

The pair met in 1973. He was twenty-three years old; she was forty-nine, a widow—her first husband dead by suicide. By all accounts they were devoted to each other. They had no children, weren't close to their families, but they had each other and for nearly four decades that was all they needed. Daniel was a long-haul trucker, and Chancey Ann rode along with him. But as the years passed, her age caught up with her, and it became more and more difficult to climb up into the truck. Her eyesight was failing, and arthritis made it hard for her to get around. Then the recession hit. The company Daniel drove for failed to pay him for months, and then it went under. His truck broke down, but there was no money to fix it. There was no money, either, for Chancey Ann's medicine for the many ailments she now suffered.

Gopshes told investigators his wife had grown up during the Depression. All too clearly, she remembered the soup and bread lines and she was terrified of reliving that. They could have put her in a nursing home, which neither wanted, and if you've spent any time around nursing homes, particularly the low-rent version, you understand why. So, in their minds that left just one choice, a suicide pact. Three times the couple tried pills, and three times they woke up. While Chancey Ann Gopshes slept on New Year's Eve, sometime around midnight Daniel Gopshes shot her in the head. If events had gone according to plan, he would have shot himself. But that's not the way it happened. When it came to his turn, Daniel Gopshes could not pull the trigger. He tried to find the courage in a bottle, but that didn't work either.

"He said he couldn't bear the thought of her body going unfound," Lincoln County DA Rob Bovett told me.

So instead of holding up his end of the pact, Gopshes called 911 and confessed. The Newport police officer found him in the cab of his truck, the .22 he'd used to shoot his wife on the front seat along with a box of ammunition. He told the officer who found him in his truck that he'd hoped the police would shoot and kill him. Instead, they arrested him on murder and the unlawful use of a weapon. The charge was later reduced to manslaughter. Gopshes pled guilty and wrote in the court papers, "(I) intentionally caused the death of Chancey Ann Gopshes while I was under the influence of extreme emotional disturbance." The judge sentenced him to ten years in prison.

As perhaps foreshadowed by those first events of New Year's, 2010 turned out to be the grayest year ever. Fog. Mist. Rain. Clouds. We couldn't buy a break, not in the weather and not in the news business, either. My colleague called to report that the new publisher was planning to make the *Oregonian* very much Portland-centric. A short time later, thirty-seven other staffers lost their jobs. It was the year I thought seriously about moving, and the year I underwent shoulder surgery.

I'm not sure how I ended up with two tears in my rotator cuff. (Steve the grocery store bagger's initial diagnosis was correct.) Surely it had something to do with the three, ninety-foot-long, four-foot-tall manor stone retaining walls we built in our back yard. My physical therapist suspected the original injury may have come from the days in my twenties when I drove a car that did not have power steering. Every so often, I'd take a turn a little too tight, catch the curb, and feel the steering wheel wretch my shoulder out of joint. It hurt like hell, but it always fixed itself.

I knew surgery would be rough, but it was arthroscopic so I figured it couldn't be that bad. Right? And initially with the nerve block and meds, it wasn't. They'd warned me to stay ahead of the pain, and I intended to try. But I hate pain meds. They make me jumpy, nauseous, dizzy. Still, I took them, charting on a notepad the hour when I took the Oxycodone and then in a couple hours the less intense Percocet and then later, again, the Oxycodone. My arm was locked tight against my body in a sling, and I was supposed to ice it throughout the day. Chan stayed home with me the first day after the surgery, then, comfortable I had matters under control, returned to work. But that first day alone, I discovered I was unable to operate the ice machine. So instead, I laid a pack of frozen vegetables on my shoulder. It started to slip, and instinctively I flipped my folded arm skyward to catch it. I saw stars, I heard howling. It wasn't until I met the dogs nose to nose that I realized I was on my knees on the floor, retching from the pain. The next day, I did it again. After that, I kept my arm tight against my body, the sling so snug my shoulder nearly touched my ear.

I missed one week of work, then worked from my laptop. I'm not sure what drove me in those days of pain, one-armed and largely sofa-bound, but I did manage to get an awful lot written. I couldn't use my right arm, so I took notes with my left hand as I talked on the phone, headset in place, fingers bobbing across the keyboard trying to keep up. In that way, I did a spring break story on Seaside, promising myself as I worked if I could just get through the story, I could take a pain pill when I was done. As much as I hated the pills, I hated the pain even worse. After the Seaside story, I did one on Lincoln City, and then interviewed eighty-one-year-old Alvin Boese, a former mechanic for the Navy, about a World War II–era warplane found by loggers on a ridge east of Rockaway Beach. It was believed to be the wreckage of a Navy Helldiver that went down in 1948. It was one of several war stories I've written that played out on the Oregon coast: including the ongoing search for a World War II submarine believed to have been sunk somewhere between Cape Meares and Cape Lookout; the World War II Japanese sub attack on Fort Stevens; and the bombing of Brookings by a sole Japanese pilot, who later became an honorary citizen of the southernmost coastal town. The Sumarai sword pilot Nobuo Fujita gave to the city hangs in the Chetco Public Library.

Months later, my shoulder finally healed and fully functioning, it was time to revisit the Bear Lady. One year had passed since Karen Noyes had been forced from her Yachats home. Her case was under appeal. After leaving Oregon, she'd gone to live with an eighty-nine-year-old friend in San Diego. One morning she went to his room to get him for breakfast and found him dead. Noyes—a senior citizen in bad health on a fixed income who'd lost a husband and daughter, as well as a pile of money over the court case—had few options. Lynn Rogers invited her to stay at his North

American Bear Center in Ely, Minnesota, and help out. That worked until Animal Planet came looking to do a story about Noyes. Rogers wanted no part of it, warning Noyes they'd "make a monkey" out of her. But Noyes wanted her story told. She moved out of the Bear Center and flew to Ohio on Animal Planet's dime for the interview. Afterward, she returned to Ely and stayed with friends, wondering if the show had been a mistake.

She sent me pictures of herself with the bears in Ely. In one she kisses a large black bear on the muzzle, in another she is bent over, inches from a bear's nose. There was a tenant living in her Yachats home, and while she would be allowed to return after three years, she said she had no interest in coming back to Oregon.

"After what happened, Tami Wagner turned the whole neighborhood against me, making the neighbors think it was my fault they had bear problems," Noyes said.

She wanted to make sure I talked about the berry freeze and the drought and how all the western states were having problems with hungry bears.

"What I want is for the bears to be righted," Noyes said. "For people to be more tolerant of bears. Here, the people are real educated. Very bear tolerant."

In October, the Animal Planet segment aired. There were pictures of some of Noyes's favorite bears, Bernadette and her daughter, who Noyes said understood her feelings. "I just told her don't go around other humans. I said I would never see her again and goodbye." Noyes also shared that she'd been abandoned by her mother at birth and raised by a woman who was cold to her. "Feeding bears has nothing to do with mental illness," Noyes said. "It's more that you want to be the good mother you never had. That's what it feels like to me."

Animal Planet did not fulfill Rogers's prediction, and instead treated her with dignity. I thought that was probably the end of the Bear Lady's story. I'd do something short when her appeal was decided and let it go at that. But months later the story took a dark twist, one that had nothing to do with bears. Before that I had a couple more animal stories to write.

It was a dreary September day when I headed to the barn at the therapeutic riding center. I figured this would be a warm, fuzzy story, not a lot of brain damage. I took my camera along since there would be no photographer coming from Portland. At the barn, I met with the program director and some of the volunteer staff. I met a mom, who brought her four boys to the barn weekly, making a two to two-and-a-half-hour trip—depending on bathroom breaks—to do so. They considered it their summer fun. The boys ranged in ages from five to nine. Three of the four boys had disabilities; three were adopted. The mom was happy to work with me, but warned me not to dare use certain language like "suffers" or "victim." Fair enough. The volunteers got the boys settled in their saddles and went to work on the skills planned for that day. Some worked outside the barn, where it was now merely dreary; others inside. I shot some photos of the riders inside, then walked out into the gray to shoot more.

I can't say what it was that first got my attention, only that suddenly there was a palpable sense of panic coming from the barn. Camera in hand, I turned to look, and doing so, found myself watching one of the most horrifying scenes I've ever witnessed: a terrified five-year-old hanging by one foot from the stirrup, his head inches from the ground, as the twelve-hundred-pound horse, also terrified, thundered around the arena trying to free herself of the screaming boy bouncing off of her side. There was a very good chance that little boy was about to be trampled under the panicked hooves of the horse. It happened in a flash, a flash that seemed to spin out forever. And then, just that quick, it was over. The boy was free; his mother—scared to death, but exuding calm—comforted him while the staff soothed the horse.

Had a professional photographer been there, I have no doubt they would have captured a shot that would have not only made A1, but likely been reprinted around the country. I not only had not so much as raised my camera. I'd turned my back, unable to watch what I was certain was going to be a tragic ending. When I returned home to write my story I didn't mention a word to my editors about the five-year-old who was very nearly crushed under the four feet of a terrified horse. Instead, I wrote about a barn in the countryside where children, some nearly blind, some crippled, some who would never age beyond the emotional maturity of a four-year-old, got the chance for a couple of hours to be just like any other kid, to feel empowered, skilled, athletic even. I did call the mom a week later. They had just returned from their weekly visit to the barn, and yes, the five-year-old was riding again.

Actress Tippi Hedren in Depoe Bay on a fundraising mission for an animal sanctuary.

Tippi Hedren greeted me in the lobby of Harbor Lights Inn in Depoe Bay impeccably dressed and looking at least a decade younger than her eighty years. On the lapel of her crushed velvet jacket was a gold pin with three pearls, a gift, she explained, from Alfred Hitchcock. She showed me to a small sitting area, as she raved about Depoe Bay. "I love this little place. We all love it," she said, referring to her family who managed the inn. Hedren was in town to host a dinner and viewing of *The Birds*, a fundraiser for the Roar Foundation's Shambala Preserve.

I flipped open my notebook and began taking notes. Now Hedren, initially gracious and warm, looked puzzled and a bit disturbed.

"But . . . no recorder?"

I explained my feelings about recorders. I didn't trust them. I suspected they made you lazy, and in the end, there was all that transcribing to do. She looked at me, still not sure, but sized me up.

"I've canceled interviews in the past when they didn't use one because I've been so misquoted," she said.

It didn't sound like a threat, so much as a concern. I promised I would call and double check on anything I was unsure of.

She shrugged. "Okay then, I guess."

From then on, Hedren was an enthusiastic subject. She told me about how she'd come to make the film *Roar*, a film that, in hindsight, might have easily gotten someone killed. It was the early 1970s, and Hedren was filming in South Africa where she became painfully aware of endangered wildlife. One day, while on a safari, they passed an abandoned house taken over by a pride of lions. "They were sitting in the windows like a portrait," she recalled.

And so began what became a ten-year odyssey to film the movie that cinematographer Randolph Sellars called, "the most dangerous movie ever made." It featured 150 lions, tigers, leopards, and cheetahs—all or most rescued from roadside zoos or private owners who realized they'd taken on more than they could handle. The movie's website states: "No animals were hurt during the filming, but 70 people were injured."

When *Roar* was finally finished, Hedren founded Shambala Preserve and gave the cats a home. Now, she had to raise $75,000 a month to keep the preserve running. "I'm broke," she told me. "As far as fundraising in this economy, I've never been this nervous and this afraid. Will I be able to come up with $75,000 or not?"

Hedren is best known for her Hollywood career, but her real passion is animals. She was a big force in pushing through legislation like the Captive Wildlife Safety Act, which bans the transportation of exotic cats across state lines. Hedren's next goal is to see a ban on breeding exotic felines for personal possession. No doubt, she'd also like to see a ban on circuses, as well.

"It's appallingly bad the way the animals are treated," she said. "The beatings of the elephants, the beatings of the cats . . . the sad way they live. . . . I don't know what the answer is. One thing is, do not go to the circus if animals are part of it.

"They tell you how well the animals are treated. They also say it's educational. What is educational about an elephant standing on its head? Or a tiger jumping through fire? What is educational about that?"

Hedren and I talked about other things that day. She is, for instance, the only female actor who worked with both Charlie Chaplin and Hitchcock, she said.

"*The Birds*, I have the attitude, how lucky I am to be able to be so involved with a film that became a classic, with the most formidable producer in the world. What is wrong with that? Nothing. The doors it opened for me were just amazing."

Hedren is also known as the godmother of the Vietnamese-American nail salon industry for her help educating Vietnamese refugees as manicurists.

But that day the conversation always came back to the animals.

"I've had a love of animals from birth," she said. "I loved getting to know other species. Every species on this Earth has a job to do. I haven't heard what the human's is. The one thing we should all be aware of is there is not one thing we can give a wild animal in captivity that they need."

Hedren called me after the story ran to thank me for getting the story right, still amazed I was able to do that without a recorder.

The official end of summer, Labor Day weekend, had come and gone on the coast. We were savoring the last glorious days of sunshine and blue sky, building up the woodpile, preparing for the gray of winter. News of the deaths came on a Saturday via an email from former news reporter Dave Dillon, who frequently tipped me off to the goings on up on his end of the coast. In the subject line: Two dead in a house in Manzanita. The note was brief: "That's the story going around. On Manzanita Ave. The street's blocked off. Cop cars everywhere. I'll send you what I know. More later."

Aside from the rash of dog poisonings back in 2004, I hadn't heard any bad news from Manzanita. And this one was a shocker—not only because no one expected this sort of thing to happen in the little village by the sea, but also because everyone knew the place where the bodies were found, the little aubergine-colored house with the lime green front door, belonged to Astrid Schlaps and Richard Hunter, owners of the art gallery ffotograffii on Laneda Avenue. The police hadn't positively identified them yet, could not positively identify them because they were so badly decomposed. If not for their clothing, they wouldn't have even been able to determine gender, they said. In any case, it was a Saturday, and I was out of hours. I handed it off to the weekend cops reporter and put it out of my mind.

On Monday, the *Oregonian* published a story identifying the couple. He was a popular professor at Portland State University. She was a newly retired licensed clinical social worker. Their house in Portland was in foreclosure. It fell to me to pick up the rest of the story, provide more details, try to solve the mystery. That was the big question—or so I thought. It would turn out to be only one of very, very many.

Schlaps was found in the living room in front of a fireplace littered with cigarette butts, and Hunter in the stairwell to the cellar. She was dressed as if to go out, and there were no lights on, leading police to theorize the shootings had occurred during the day. Initially, police said she'd been shot in the front of the head, which turned out to be wrong. She had been shot from behind. They also reported there were groceries just purchased and left in the car, though it was later decided they were not newly bought groceries, but likely food they were taking back to their Portland home. Talk around town was that Schlaps was battling a terminal illness and people theorized that it had been a mercy killing, a suicide pact.

I began making calls to people in Manzanita and discovered early on that pretty much everyone knew them and everyone, it seemed, liked them. Without fail, friends talked about the great love the two shared. They were devoted to each other. Everyone said so. They married in 2007 in a wedding that began at the Pine Grove Community Center, which the pair had decorated with fabric and lights. From the community center, a crowd of close to one hundred friends and family walked down Laneda Avenue to the beach, where the pair handed out paper parasols. A friend performed the wedding service. Schlaps and Hunter recited vows from "The Owl and the Pussycat," and another friend made a ceremonial dive into the ocean. Then, they gathered in tents to hoist champagne.

Three years later, they were set to live full time on the Oregon coast—a dream they'd nurtured for years. And the foreclosure in Portland? It didn't matter, friends said. They were glad to be rid of it. All that mattered was living the good life by the sea.

My first story ran four days after the bodies were found. The emails and phone calls poured in. No one believed Hunter murdered Schlaps and then committed suicide, except the investigators. The Manzanita police and the Tillamook County Sheriff's office were in charge of the investigation, and they were ready to close the case. They had the weapon and the two bullets fired from it. They had the medical examiner's findings, which supported their theory and also revealed that Schlaps had not had any serious life-threatening illnesses. That, it seemed, was that.

But it was not. Bonnie and Richard Speer, a couple who lived close by, wrote to tell me of celebrating Hunter's birthday on August 26, and of a visit they made to the couple's Portland house months earlier when Hunter had given them an antique family phonograph. In the note, Bonnie, who owned an art framing shop in Nehalem, numbered ten reasons why it could not have been a murder-suicide or suicide pact, including, "Astrid abhorred suicide. . . . She talked people out of it for twenty-five years."

One curious encounter haunted Bonnie. On September 1, she'd run into Hunter at the local grocery store. They hugged and talked of what a good time they'd had at the dinner party the week before. Looking back, what bothered her was that Hunter seemed to be in a hurry. "Richard was never in a hurry," Bonnie said. He told her they had company coming, and he wasn't looking forward to it.

The story was starting to nag me. I knew too many details, and much of it made no sense. After hearing of Bonnie's last encounter with Hunter, I began to wonder, Was Schlaps already dead? Had Hunter shot her, then sat there smoking, working up the courage to take the next step?

But Bonnie didn't believe Hunter had pulled the trigger.

"I knew these people. I knew them better than most people here did. She was retiring, and she was so happy to be coming down here. When she closed her practice, she had me frame twenty pictures as gifts for clients she cared about. Any one of those clients would have known where her house was. She had this one couple that gave her hell after she said she was going to retire. These people would not let her go. They were ugly, and they were threatening."

The Speers and others pleaded with me to please convince the police not to close the investigation. There were too many oddities. Why was the door locked? They never locked their door because they were always going outside to smoke. Why were their two cats, pets they treated like children, locked inside? And where did the gun come from? Everyone knew they were antigun. Others also emailed me or called, as well as posted comments on the *Oregonian*'s website. One former student questioned why there was no note and why two such intelligent, loving people would take violent actions that would cause trauma to the thousands whose lives they touched.

But despite the many inconsistencies, the doubts, the absolute certainty this couldn't be what it appeared, the sheriff, the police chief, and others believed it was clearly murder-suicide. Mostly, so did I. But I promised to at least raise the questions.

By then, I had a better relationship with Tillamook County Sheriff Todd Anderson than anybody I worked with on the coast. We had become so friendly that I'd call him and say, "Hey, it's me." And he knew exactly who "me" was. Anderson occasionally humored me about my naivete. Once, I'd received calls from several people in Florida whose friend was missing and had last been heard from after calling from the north coast to say he'd been mugged and all his money taken. They were sure he'd met with foul play and begged me to do a story. I went to Anderson, who listened and chuckled and shared that they got such calls all the time and usually the missing person was partying with the locals and not interested in being found. "But Todd," I'd said, "these people are convinced. This guy wouldn't do something like that." Finally, Anderson, probably sick of my phone calls, agreed to do some looking. Moments later, he called to say they had pinged the missing man's phone, and as he'd predicted, found him hanging out in a park with some of the locals.

But this was different. Two people, reportedly very much in love with each other, were inexplicably dead. As promised, I called Anderson and Manzanita police Chief Erik Harth and raised the questions that had been put to me. They listened. They explained their reasoning. I'd done what I could. I was ready to leave the matter alone and let them handle the criticism and questions.

Then, one day after my story ran, I walked into my office and found an email from another of the couple's close friends. And suddenly, I was one of the nonbelievers.

> Dear Lori.
> I think you should see this. I just found out the name of the woman who was helping Astrid and Richard move, the one the cops didn't think to check out. Her name was ____ _____.
> This link (below) is the story of her past criminal history. I'm sorry, but can this be just a coincidence? Please ask the sheriff to find and interrogate her on where she was, etc., on the day of the murder. We know that Astrid was complaining about this woman a week or so before this happened.
> G.

I clicked on the link and found a story the *Oregonian* had published in 2008 about a woman who had duct taped her estranged partner to a chair, shoved a gun to her neck, and talked about killing her ex-partner and then herself. The woman was sentenced to one year and a day in prison. She had served her sentence and was out. She had a key to the couple's Manzanita house and a crush, friends said, on Schlaps.

First thing in the morning, I called Anderson. And this time, I could tell by the silence that he was now wondering, too. A short time later, he called to tell me he had contacted the woman and would be traveling to Portland to interview her. Harth also agreed to keep investigating.

Meanwhile, the notes continued, as did the posts on a memorial website started in honor of the couple. One wrote: "Astrid was an astounding, compassionate human being and therapist. She was truly gifted, bestowed her gifts on many, and was a treasure in my life." Another wrote: "Astrid was a bright, open, caring, and humble person . . . so knowledgeable and talented." Of Hunter, someone wrote: "To me, Richard was a kind, gentle, and soft spoken man. . . . May we remember the man that we all knew Richard to be. . . . He will be missed." When printed, the comments on the website filled thirty-odd pages. But not everyone wrote in praise of Richard Hunter.

In an email to me, one former student and neighbor wrote, "At one point in the 1990s while they were both professors, Richard ran off with a . . . student. I believe he even moved in with her for a while. Astrid was totally devastated. Then she ultimately took him back. . . . Many people seem to want to frame this as a mercy killing. Personally, I see it as something more sinister."

Another wrote to say that Hunter had once nearly driven them to financial ruin, but Schlaps was able to save them thanks to an inheritance from her mother.

I was getting so many calls, so many questions, that my editors agreed to let me do another story. This would make three in the seven days since the bodies were found. I was able to reach Tillamook medical examiner Paul Betlinski. He had not performed the autopsies, but was involved in the onsite investigation.

"Double homicide, that is the question that always arises," he said. "Is this a possibility? I do not see how this could have been a double homicide. From the position of the body, the position of the gun."

He also talked about the scene, and his own instincts about what happened on that day sometime after September 1.

"Everything is very consistent with his being the user of the gun in both cases," Betlinski said. "The consistence with the entry wound on the head and the trajectory. As if she was looking off to one side and her head bowed down as if getting something out of her purse or off the table. Hers was in the back of the head as if someone came up behind her. His was a temple entry, pretty much going straight across as if someone was holding a gun against his own head. Both were in slumped positions. She was sitting in the living room, laying back on the couch. Her purse was open and there was a five-dollar bill in her fingertips. She may have just come in and sat on the couch. He was on the stairs going down to the basement. He had removed himself from the living room . . .

"In my mind, I don't see how anyone else could have put a pistol where he was, and killed him without his cooperation. . . . I am very comfortable she did not kill herself. I can't tell you if she was complicit or not. My suspicion was that she was not aware that this was happening. I am still puzzling over the whole thing myself."

As were so many other people. The third story ran, prompting another reader to write about a woman who admired Schlaps to obsessive levels. "She imitated her style of dress and emulated her to a crazy degree. She went on to do other obsessive acts not worth mentioning here, but I saw it as a response to her tremendous personal power. . . . I could see the woman who imitated her obsessively stalking her—and if she was psychotic, perhaps killing them."

Someone else pointed out that five dollars was the usual insurance co-pay for a visit with a therapist. Had Schlaps been expecting a former patient?

Three more weeks passed before the investigation was closed. The woman who'd spent time in prison for threatening her partner had a solid alibi, and police now had Hunter's cell phone records as well as thorough interviews with anyone who might have been involved or in contact with the couple around the time of the crime. Harth went to great lengths to answer all the questions, aware, I am sure, that if he did not complete an exhaustive investigation, it would go down forever more as the double homicide investigators botched, the perpetrator never caught.

In early October, Harth called to tell me what they had learned. The antigun couple were apparently not quite as opposed to weapons as friends believed. Hunter had purchased the .357 and .38 caliber bullets in Tillamook in January that same year. Schlaps had told a friend they bought the gun for protection when Hunter was teaching in Portland and she was alone in Manzanita. The cigarettes in the fireplace came from the couple, who smoked outside, then brought the butts inside. Autopsy x-rays had shown that each had died of a single bullet wound to the head. And thanks to phone records and interviews with the family, police now had what seemed a solid answer to the question of why.

Not only was the house in Portland in foreclosure, but the couple was six months behind on an interest-only loan on the Manzanita house, and had substantial credit card debt. "There were voice mails left at Richard's work," Harth said. "There's one on August 31 that said every option expired at 6:00 p.m. today. There is one on August 27 at 12:30 p.m. that says you only have until August 31 at 6:30 p.m. There were at least five different creditors that had left messages at his work phone in a ten-day period. From what I've learned in my investigation, Astrid did not know about the current financial problems."

The story had gotten to me. I couldn't get past the fact that a woman so happy in her life, a woman so loved and admired by so many, had had her life stolen from her by the one man she should have been able to trust most. Of course, those were the feelings I was not allowed to write. And so I wrote one final news story on Schlaps and Hunter, glad that this tale was done. Or so I thought. Months would pass before I found myself enmeshed in their story again in one of the eeriest coincidences I've experienced.

Maryanne lived in New Jersey and was a neighbor and very close friend of my cousin. She contacted me that fall wondering if I had written about Kelli Hawthorne. I had not. I'd never even heard of Hawthorne. I reminded Maryanne that the Oregon coast is 360 miles long, so odds were whatever had happened to this person probably hadn't been near me.

Maryanne wrote back. Was I by chance close to Gleneden Beach? Close? I live roughly twelve miles away.

I assumed this person was someone Maryanne knew, but as it turned out she had only read about the New Jersey girl in the local newspaper. She sent me a link to the story about a young woman's desire to see the stars on the Oregon coast and how that wish one year earlier had nearly killed her. Hawthorne, a pretty blond with brown eyes, a lovely smile, and the personality to match, was in Gleneden Beach for her brother's September 2009 wedding. It was late at night and Hawthorne realized she hadn't been on the beach yet.

"It was so dark," she recalled. "I wanted to go to the beach because the stars were so bright. I'd never seen it like that before." That's as much as Hawthorne remembers. Her friend Evan Alexander told me the rest. The pair decided to take a walk down to the beach and set out on what looked like a gravel path but was in fact just decoration. By the time Alexander realized it wasn't a path, Hawthorne was already moving beyond it.

"She thought it was a grassy slope," he said. "There was kind of like a gasp. It happened too quickly for her to do anything. I couldn't see what happened; it was too dark. I kept calling her name, and I couldn't hear anything back. I went to the edge."

That's when he saw how big of a drop-off it was.

"I got sick to my stomach. I saw her feet first. She was entirely upside down, wedged face first in the rocks. I was pretty sure she was dead."

Using the light from his cell phone, Alexander made his way to the rocks below. "I felt I needed to at least find her first. I called 911. She started to regain consciousness. She was trying to move, and I kept trying to get her not to move. She was trying to get herself out. She managed to get her legs around the rock that was up against her chest—sort of like an upside down pretzel. She was stuck even worse than she had been. There was no getting her out."

Rescuers worked for hours to move the boulders so they could safely help her.

"Every time I think of her disappearing over the edge I get sick to my stomach," Alexander said.

Hawthorne's mom, Ruth, calls her daughter a miracle. She broke both arms, the fingers on her right hand, her clavicle, and seven ribs. She shattered her jaw, knocked out four teeth, and suffered a lacerated liver and traumatic brain injury. Doctors used the inside of her cheeks to reconstruct her mouth and a piece of bone from her chin to start a bone graft. She would also need a gum graft and a permanent cheek replacement.

I finished the story, awed by Hawthorne's courage and the family's gratitude to the medical team who cared for her at Legacy Emanuel Medical Center in Portland. Hawthorne still faced a great deal of surgery and therapy and was already looking at $150,000 in medical debt. Her family hoped that by getting the word out about her plight they might warn others away from the same fate, and perhaps figure out a way to help raise funds for her debt.

The next day, Hawthorne's story ran on the metro cover, and I treated myself that afternoon to a pedicure. As my feet soaked, I talked about my day with the salon owner, including, of course, about Hawthorne. From across the room, a woman spoke up, "You wrote this?" she said, holding up the *Oregonian*. "I did," I said. She crossed the room and introduced herself. She was a TV reporter visiting the Oregon coast from New Jersey. And, like the rest of us, always on the hunt for a good story.

Nearly a decade later, in the course of writing this book, I caught up with Kelli. She had recently married and over the year undergone more reconstructive surgery. She still deals with the effects of traumatic brain injury. And yet, this positive young woman who is now the mother of twin girls showed no hint of self-pity.

"Since I got married, I moved to Long Beach Island, New Jersey, and live at the beach!" Kelli wrote. "Thankfully, for me, the beaches are very, very different than those on the West Coast."

It was time for our annual trip to Seattle. Chan would go to a Seahawks game; I would shop, then meet him at the Bookstore Bar. It's become one of my favorite trips of the year. But that year when we made the five-plus hour drive, I was plagued with a sense of impending doom, on edge the entire drive. I chalked it up to all the stress and bad news in my life, combined with the years of small-town living. I was no longer used to freeway driving and the volume, the speeds, the jackass drivers tended to unnerve me.

That year, my friend Mary, a.k.a. my former editor from the *Rocky*, and our friend Judy met us there. We took them to Pike Place Market, for French cuisine at Maximilien's, and over to Anthony's for oyster shooters they don't normally offer but improvised with shots of pepper vodka for us.

On Monday, Chan and I began the journey home. It was an uneventful drive—four-plus hours of freeway driving, followed by an hour or so traveling the last leg on the curving, narrow Highway 20, so notorious for its deadly accidents cars once sported bumper stickers reading, "Pray for me. I Drive Highway 20." (The deadliest stretch would eventually be realigned at a cost of $368 million, more than double the original estimate, and open in 2016, seven years after the original predicted completion date of 2009.)

Ten miles from home, we saw accident detour signs and rerouted off the highway through the back roads around Toledo. When we came out at the next intersection with Highway 20, I looked to the east and saw the twisted pile of metal that resembled nothing I could name. "Oh Chan," I said. "I don't know what happened, but it's bad." About the same time, I got the police alert on my phone warning of a fatal accident and detour on the road.

Once home, in the middle of unpacking, I forgot all about it. Early Tuesday morning, the phone rang. I picked it up and found my breaking news team colleague on the other end, asking, "Did you hear about the fatal accident on Highway 20?"

"We passed it on the way home yesterday," I said.

"I posted a brief," she said. "I figured since you worked with her you'd want to write the story about the woman from Fish and Wildlife who was killed."

And that was how I learned that Tami Wagner, the woman who may very well have saved the Bear Lady's life, was dead.

My mom was set to turn eighty the first week of November. We knew she wouldn't be with us all that much longer. Like me, she had had shoulder surgery. But she never fully recovered. Instead, she began the decline that we knew would never really get better. Prior to the surgery my mother had been a vibrant seventy-nine-year-old. Granted, she was overweight and had begun using a cane and sometimes a walker, and her shoulders were all but useless, though she had some use of her arms. Prior to her surgery, she told me in the cheerful voice of one heading for a vacation on the beach, "The doctor's going to repair one shoulder. I'll go to rehab for six weeks, and then I'll get out, and they'll do the other shoulder." She envisioned her rehabilitation in a newer facility, the sort of place an athlete might go for physical therapy. Instead, she nearly died from an infection, and when she did come out of the hospital, she was a frail, wheelchair-bound elderly woman, destined to spend the bulk of her remaining days in a nursing home—the kind populated not by elite athletes but by equally declining men and women who no doubt longed to be anyplace else. She'd made a mistake, an irrevocable one, and she knew it. I've never stopped asking myself what kind of surgeon thinks it is a smart idea to do elective surgery on a morbidly obese woman. And to add insult to injury, there was nothing they could do for her shoulder. There was simply nothing left to work with. Shouldn't they have figured that out before opening her up?

Readying for my trip back East, I packed my suitcase, tucking my Canon Rebel and lens deep within my clothing, knowing as I did that I was asking for trouble. It seemed any time I packed the camera a few days early, a story broke, and I was stuck scrambling to unpack it. But it had been a quiet week, so quiet, I was feeling guilty about not getting enough done.

The info alert from the Oregon State Police (OSP) came in at 2:30 p.m. There'd been a drowning at the Yaquina Bay jetty. I was leaving in the morning, but this was my backyard. It wasn't something I could ignore. I filed a brief, retrieved the Rebel, and raced to the jetty. There are two jetties at Yaquina Bay, the north and the south. At the time, the north was blocked but not the south, and you could walk clear to the end. The jetties are meant to provide safe navigation for vessels transiting the bar out to sea, but they are also a rocky link to the open ocean that people can't seem to resist. The south jetty stretches more than a mile. It begins as an easy enough walk over sand and earth, but soon leads to exposed boulders, some as big as thirty to fifty tons in size. To traverse these requires hopping, crawling, and climbing from boulder to boulder. They are slick, with crevices between them and nothing to hold on to. I wouldn't walk to the end of the jetty on the calmest, flattest day of the year. That day, the seas were breaking across the jetties at twenty feet with white frothy-looking waves that seemed ominous even on dry land.

By the time I arrived, most everyone was gone. There was an OSP pickup truck with a pair of bicycles in the bed. Larry Coonrod from the *Newport News-Times* was still hanging around and, bless his generous soul, pointed out to me an eyewitness and explained that a second witness, no longer at the scene, was visiting from British Columbia.

I approached the man Coonrod had identified, and he shared his story with me. Larry Prantl often walked on the jetty in calm conditions, but even then he never went out more than halfway. On that November day, Prantl had sat on the rocks and felt the waves shaking the jetty. They were coming in from the northwest and breaking all the way across from north to south. "I've never seen it that way," he said.

He passed Katie and Mike Myers heading out as he walked in. They were thirty-three and thirty-four years old respectively and visiting the coast to celebrate their fifteenth anniversary. He figured they'd soon turn around. But when he turned to watch their progress, they were still headed toward the sea. Even as they started getting wet from the spray, they kept going. When the pair disappeared, Prantl asked a woman to call 911, and in a short time, the rescue-turned-recovery efforts were under way.

Katie Myers's body had already been found. The Coast Guard was still looking for Mike. After I heard the story, I asked an Oregon State Trooper if there was any indication the pair had been suicidal. I wasn't being sarcastic; I honestly couldn't imagine why anyone would think that was a safe thing to do. He said he'd had the same thought, but there was no note, no reason to think they had a death wish. In the parking lot at the South Beach State Park adjacent to the south jetty, I found a van with British Columbia license plates. I left my business card under the wiper blade and in the door.

At home, it wasn't long before the phone rang, and I found the second eyewitness on the other end. George Bulawka, forty-eight, was supposed to be on his way home to Vancouver, British Columbia, Wednesday, but the weather in Newport that day was so nice, he couldn't bring himself to leave just yet. Instead, he drove out to the jetty, thinking he might take a walk to the end. But although it was a blue sky, mild day, Bulawka could tell the jetty wasn't a safe place to be.

He was resting on the beach near the jetty when a wave came in and soaked him. When he stood, he spotted the pair. They'd just parked their bikes and were walking out the jetty. Bulawka, a schoolteacher, thought the pair looked like they had clambered over such boulders before. They looked fit. When they neared the end, he assumed there must be some shelter there, some safe place. He was wrong.

"I have pretty good eyesight, and I saw a taller person, I assumed to be the man, holding on to the white pole. I could see another person crouched down behind him. I saw several waves coming over and he was still holding on, and the next wave they were gone."

Bulawka's voice broke as he spoke, and for a moment I feared mine would, too. Only weeks earlier, I'd had my first evaluation since joining the *Oregonian*. The only real criticism, if it could be called that, was that I tended to get too emotionally involved with my stories. My editor was concerned that because I worked alone, unlike my colleagues in the newsroom, I didn't have others around to unload on.

That afternoon, as my editor and I discussed the story, I heard my voice break as I described Bulawka's sorrow. Then realizing what I was doing, I stopped myself and made a lighthearted quip.

But here's what happens with that kind of story. You're on deadline. You have a story to report, facts to find, eyewitnesses to interview. Photos to shoot. You know it's an incredibly tragic story. You know two people are

Flowers mark the Yachats site where two students were swept to their deaths.

dead and needlessly so, but the demands of the day trump your emotions and you go on. But it always catches up with you. At least it did with me. Often it would come as Chan and I relaxed before the TV. There'd we be having a perfectly nice night and suddenly there it was in my face.

At three that morning, I awoke and sat straight up, thinking of them, those lone bicycles in the back of the pickup. When the tears started, I let them roll 'til they lulled me back to sleep.

Three months after the Myers died, two South Eugene High School students, Connor Ausland, eighteen, and Jack Harnsongkram, seventeen, at the coast for a weekend retreat, were washed off the rocks in Yachats, bringing, as far as we could count, the number of people washed off beaches, jetties, and oceanside rocks to fourteen in little more than a decade.

After the death of Katie and Mike Myers, the US Army Corps of Engineers blocked access to the south jetty, cementing in posts and running a chain across the path. Someone hooked a truck to it and yanked it out.

EIGHT

HEROES

2011

On our first trip to San Pedro on Belize's Ambergris Caye, I carried a new smartphone that I hadn't quite figured out fully how to use. With an aging and ailing mom, and one pup at home with the dog sitter, I couldn't just cut ties with the world. I planned to limit my visits to the hotel computer to check emails only once a day, but I needed to know if someone was trying to reach me they'd get through. So the cell phone stayed on. And so did the alarms and alerts I hadn't figured out how to turn off. In the wee hours of the morning the phone started buzzing. I was still on Oregon time, not sleeping well in a new place, and I couldn't resist checking to see what was going on. The info alert said something about a cop shooting in Lincoln County. The news registered with me and yet not quite. I was still waking up. Then the phone rang for real.

"Hey, it's Kimberly," said my colleague from the Portland newsroom. "I hear there's some excitement in your neck of the woods."

"I know, I just saw that."

"Well, how soon do you think you can be there?"

"Not very. I'm in Belize."

And that was how I missed one of the biggest manhunts ever to take place on the central coast. Shortly before 11:00 p.m., Lincoln City Police Officer Steve Dodds had stopped a Dodge Ram on the edge of town. The driver, David Durham, fired multiple shots at him, critically wounding him in the stomach, and sped off. Dodds managed to radio for help. Across the highway and at home in bed, volunteer fireman Bob Duby saw the page—"Officer down"—grabbed his first responder kit and ran to help.

There was a time missing such a big story would have cast a shadow on my sun-filled vacation, but I was falling in love. On Ambergris Caye, my head cleared, my heart slowed. With the exception of the once-a-day visit, I stayed away from the computer and looked at the phone only to ensure that family members or the dog sitter were not trying to reach me.

Even with those efforts, work was never very far away. One evening at the pool, I met Pat and Richard. They had a second home in Rockaway Beach and were, sadly enough, all too familiar with my byline. In 2005, I had written the brief when their son-in-law and grandson's small boat capsized on Nehalem Bay on New Year's Eve. Their grandson saved himself by clawing his way up on the rocks. Their son-in-law died.

I returned from vacation to find the manhunt still going strong and my help needed. I drove to Waldport to interview Lincoln County Deputy Abby Dorsey, credited with stopping Durham's 1984 Dodge SUV. She'd been asleep when the call came at about 11:30 p.m. from 911 dispatchers. She threw on sweats and her bulletproof vest and hurried out into the night. The car chase, with speeds up to eighty miles per hour, was now just miles north of her. Newport Police Sergeant Tony Garbarino warned her by radio that they were taking shots and to be careful. Dorsey parked by the side of the road, then raced across Highway 101 to set the six-foot-long spike strip on the fog line where it wouldn't snag an innocent passerby. Crouched in the ditch, Dorsey listened as the sirens, the only sound in the night, grew closer, then moments before Durham's SUV passed, yanked the spike strip into place. After hearing the SUV hit it, she again yanked the strip off the highway so police wouldn't do the same.

Durham jumped from the SUV and ran into the woods above Alsea Bay. They searched for him in vacant homes, sheds, and boats. They looked on horseback, by plane, boat, and helicopter but, save for his dog, not another sign of Durham was found. The dog was returned to the family. After months in the hospital, Dodds survived.

A month later, a female hiker from Waldport also went missing, not far from where Durham was last seen. For a moment I had to wonder, but when I voiced my thoughts to the police the deputy asked what I was smoking. It didn't seem so far-fetched to me. Durham was a camper, an outdoorsman, depending who you asked. How odd would have it been for him to have been holed up in the woods and inadvertently stumbled upon by a hiker? She was also never found. Her dog, however, like Durham's, turned up at a home not far from where she was last seen.

One of the problems of living in a small town for any period of time is that there are few people you aren't somehow connected with, which suggests a certain built-in bias one way or the other, no matter how hard you try to avoid it. Much of the world knew Dr. Steve Brown as the veterinarian to Keiko, the resident orca for a time at the Oregon Coast Aquarium. But to me, he was just the guy I ran to anytime one of my pets needed care. Over the years, I learned of some fun, mostly feel-good stories from Dr. Brown. It was to my editors' credit that they understood that much as I was a staff writer for the *Oregonian*, I was also still a part of the community. I still had a personal life. And so, once in a while, I'd hear of something interesting in the animal kingdom, and they'd let me write about it.

Once, Dr. Brown told me about a dog who had seen two small dogs struggling in the surf. Their owner had died while walking them, and they remained tangled in their leashes, still attached to his body. Had it not been for the efforts of this "hero" canine to call his owner's attention to the two, they surely would have drowned. While working on that story, Dr. Brown invited me on his rounds at the Oregon Coast Aquarium, where he worked with marine mammals to keep them healthy. I was completely in awe as he put one of the seals through her paces—enticing her to stand against the wall, flippers spread. She thought she was doing a trick for which there would be a handsome reward, and she was, but the real purpose was to allow Dr. Brown to physically examine her.

While I watched him at work at the aquarium, he told me about Aialik, a sea otter orphaned and rescued from Alaska. Aialik had a chronic bladder infection.

Now several years later, Dr. Brown was freshly recovered from pancreatic cancer, and I was peering through the window of his operating room as he prepared to do an unprecedented surgery on the sea otter. For the past thirteen months, Aialik had not been able to urinate on his own without a catheter and suffered chronic infections that could eventually make

Dr. Steven Brown puts Candy through her paces during an exam.

him seriously ill or even lead to his death. In the past year, they'd replaced the catheter five times. They needed a different approach.

Dr. Brown and his team planned to attach Aialik's bladder to his abdominal wall, then marsupialize it. That is, they would create a hole in the bladder wall from which urine could leak. The hole was expected to heal to about the size of the tip of a pen. I was invited to watch the surgery.

First, they sedated Aialik. Then, with a cone over his face, they administered the anesthesia. At 9:20 a.m., they raced the limp animal into the operating room and went to work. Fast. The longer the animal is under, the bigger the risk. Aialik's heart could have gone into fibrillation or his blood pressure taken a dangerous drop or any number of unforeseen problems could have arisen. So, the veterinarians gave themselves just 120 minutes to get the job done.

Outside the operating room, I was joined by vet techs and visiting guests from the Oregon State University (OSU) veterinary school watching as the team of doctors worked. From the kennels in the back, the occasional meow or bark could be heard from recuperating animals. Partway through the procedure, Aialik stirred. "Steen," Dr. Brown called out for the vet tech. Steen rushed in, ready with more anesthesia.

At 10:47 a.m., with just minutes to spare on the stopwatch, Aialik was wheeled to recovery. Less than three hours later, the sea otter was on his way back to the aquarium.

We had made it through the winter without any significant storms and were now headed into spring, thankful, as most here are, that sunnier skies were surely on the way. But at nearly midnight on a Thursday the phones started ringing. I was in bed. I didn't hear the landline and by the time I got upstairs to my cell, it had gone to voicemail. Then Chan's cell rang. I picked up mine and returned the call to the newsroom. A mega earthquake had struck Japan; a tsunami was expected to hit the Oregon coast at about 7:00 a.m.

We take our tsunamis seriously here in Oregon—at least the media and people in the business of safety do. There are also those as likely to go to the beach to watch for a tsunami as they are to get to high ground. But that is changing, too, as is the way we react to tsunamis. In recent years scientists have begun to understand the reality of the Cascadia Subduction Zone—the fracture in the earth off our coast that will someday devastate the Pacific Northwest with a mega earthquake. The last time it occurred was in 1700, and it is estimated that thousands likely died from the quake and tsunami that followed. Three hundred years is a long time, long enough to make it difficult for many to take the threat seriously. But Newport has a much more recent tragic history with tsunamis.

In 1964, when a magnitude 9.2 earthquake hit Alaska on Good Friday, my husband was five years old. He remembers watching cartoons, then the house shaking, the kitchen cupboard doors banging. He and his family ran out of the house as it slid off the foundation.

At 11:30 that same night, a ten-foot tsunami wave crashed over Beverly Beach on the central Oregon coast. The McKenzie family was camping there, tucked in sleeping bags in a driftwood shelter. In various news reports repeated over the years, Monte McKenzie, an engineer with Boeing, recalled the water filling their shelter to within a foot of the top, the children screaming. Rita McKenzie described holding two of the children by the hands and then not. She was knocked unconscious by a log. The four children were swept out to sea. Only one body was recovered. Seaside and Cannon Beach flooded; bridges and homes were damaged or washed away. One woman died of a heart attack. She just happened to be sitting in a car outside city hall waiting to evacuate when the emergency siren blared. In Crescent City on the north California coast, ten people died and the town was largely washed away.

In 2004, I was only seven months into the job when I sat in on a conference at the Inn at Otter Rock and listened to people share their memories of the 1964 tsunami. The Indian Ocean tsunami had just wiped out entire populations and suddenly everyone was talking about what might happen here, what happened once before.

In 1964, Kathleen Clark, a featured speaker at the conference, was a college sophomore on spring break with her family in Neskowin. All evening, as Clark and her family waited for the wave to hit, they listened to the ocean roaring outside their cottage. Then, she recalled, suddenly the ocean went silent.

"There wasn't any sound, no ocean," Clark told the audience gathered that night. She looked out the window. There were no waves, no shine from the moon. A minute passed, then another. And then came a noise like a freight train, and a wall of water thundered toward land, crashing over the seawall and into the front yard of the cottage. Clark, her boyfriend, and brother watched the ocean withdraw, sucking far, far out, and again the night grew silent. The second even bigger wave followed, and after that, a third. "And then, it was over," she said.

As Clark watched the news accounts of the Indian Ocean tsunami, she understood the fascination that kept some eyewitnesses transfixed and frozen when they should have been racing to save their own lives. She had done the same thing.

"We didn't run, we didn't head for higher ground," she said. "We just sat and watched."

Now, seven years later, the Oregon coast was again the target of a distant-generated tsunami. Would it be a no-show, as others had been, or would we experience the devastation of 1964?

I told my editors I'd get some sleep, and then head out in the wee hours. At about four in the morning, I saw alerts on my cell indicating they were evacuating people. Chan set out for the PUD—at the time located in an inundation zone and across the only bridge linking Newport to the south and South Beach to the north—to get the line trucks to higher ground. I jumped in my RAV and headed out. On any other morning at that hour, the coast would have been dark and empty, but on that morning Highway 101 glowed with the flow of lights from RVs, trailered boats, cars, and pickups, all bound inland. The gas stations were doing a brisk business; a fire station in Gleneden Beach opened to offer shelter to those being evacuated. I drove north to talk to the evacuees, aware as I drove past Beverly Beach that if a tsunami of any size struck, I could be cut off from home.

At about 6:00 a.m., *Oregonian* photographer Ben Brink called to let me know he had arrived in town. I told him to meet me at Yaquina Bay lighthouse, where we'd be high enough to be safe, but also have a perfect view of the bay and the ocean. Everyone else in Newport had the same idea. Remembering Kathleen Clark's tale, I was expecting the drama of the ocean receding, then roaring back, crashing over the beach. And so there we stood, watching, waiting. Soon, we took our eyes off the ocean. We talked, we caught up with friends we hadn't seen for a while, introduced ourselves to people we just met. As we talked, 7:00 a.m. came and went, and soon it was 8:00 a.m., and the ocean looked just like it always had. Little by little the crowd disappeared. I called the newsroom to report the nonevent, and Ben and I went our separate ways.

It was a Friday. I was out of hours and ready for the weekend. But the story was far from over. I just didn't know it yet. It would be some time before I learned the tsunami had not been a nonevent everywhere. One young man, who drove to the beach with friends to watch the tsunami in northern California near the Klamath River, was swept out to sea. Crescent City, just recovering from a tsunami generated by an earthquake in the Kuril Islands in 2006, saw its harbor once again destroyed. Brookings suffered $7 million in damage and lost eighteen thousand square feet of commercial dock. In Depoe Bay, twelve miles north of Newport, a wave rolled in, picking up a boat and dropping it back down on the dock. The little town lost forty feet of dock. Even here in Newport, people who watched closely saw the ocean change.

"The tide would go all the way out to like at least a minus 2.9 tide, but even lower," Sylvia Beach Hotel innkeeper Charlotte Dinolt told me. "It was really, really out. Then, it moved in really quickly all the way to the bank. The creepy part was there were no waves, and it was a weird color. It went on for a long time, just ebb and pull, ebb and pull. It was not a normal ocean at all. It just sloshed back and forth. It was a little unnerving for everybody."

A month later, my story on the devastation expected in Oregon when (scientists insist it's not if) the Cascadia Subduction Zone ruptures ran as the centerpiece on A1. At about 10:00 a.m., my phone rang. After many years of reporting, I could tell almost from the first word whether a call would be a good call or one I wished I hadn't picked up. This one sounded like the latter.

"Are you the reporter responsible for this morning's front-page news story?" he asked.

"I am."

"Well thanks . . ."

Ok, I thought, maybe I had this one wrong.

". . . for ruining my business. I will never buy another *Oregonian* again." Click.

After the Manzanita murder-suicide, I promised Bonnie and Richard Speer that I would stop by their gallery in Nehalem and meet them. I also thought I would drive by the house where Richard Hunter killed Astrid Schlaps before taking his own life. The whole dark event haunted me, and I thought seeing the place might give me some kind of closure. But although I'd made numerous trips north in those ten or so months since it happened, I didn't stop in to introduce myself, nor did I drive by the scene of the crime. I still thought about it a lot.

Chan's birthday falls in early June, just after Memorial Day but before school's out. It was something of a local secret at the time that in that week the coast was still largely empty of visitors, the weather summery, and the prices not quite up to high season levels yet. We rented a room in our usual spot across from the ocean, loaded up our terrier/boxer rescue Mugsy, and Friday afternoon, headed north. The weekend was completely open, except for one visit I felt compelled to finally make: to meet Bonnie and Richard Speer. They had been a huge help to me in writing about the tragedy, and I felt I owed them a personal thanks. Even more so, like many others I'd met through tragedy, they had become my friends. We talked occasionally by phone and emailed often as we continued to make sense of what had happened in that little eggplant-colored house on that summer day.

Saturday dawned unusually warm for a coast morning. At 10:00 a.m. when we set out for Nehalem it was already in the seventies. Chan pulled out of the motel parking lot and started toward 101.

"Wait," I shouted. "Turn left here. I want to see if I can spot the house."

I didn't have to say any more. He knew what house. I knew the street it was on and that it had an odd colored front door, though I didn't remember exactly what color it was. About two blocks along, I spotted a cottage with a bright purple door. "That must be it," I said. I had expected some sort of connection. But oddly, I felt nothing. Still, now I would let it go.

About three blocks farther, I spotted an estate sale. When we were young and broke and living in Connecticut, we spent entire Saturdays visiting "tag" sales. I loved the possibility of finding some treasure at a bargain basement price. Once, we bought a huge old early model microwave for forty dollars. It lasted us years. I bought three antique typewriters over the years and never paid more than fifteen dollars for any of them, and I still use the vintage Pyrex dishes from those outings. It had been some time since I'd been to an estate sale, but I was tempted. In a place like Manzanita where many homes are second homes, owned by people with money, the odds of finding quality items is good.

I told Chan to stop, but then changed my mind. "It's too hot for Mugsy," I said.

"You go ahead," he said. "I'll park in the shade."

"I still think it's too warm," I said.

"Then I'll stay out here with him and leave the A/C on."

So off I went. The front door was open, the sale doing a brisk and steady business. I walked into the living room, where a table was piled with all sorts of things: china, books, dinnerware. I reminded myself I didn't need any of it, but couldn't resist picking up a small piece of art. It was a cityscape framed in a deep border of bronze. I turned it over and felt my stomach clutch. The label on the back read: ffotograffii. It couldn't be. My legs grew wobbly; my hands shook. Across the room was the fireplace. I remembered that Schlaps had been sitting on a sofa opposite a fireplace when she was shot.

I went in search of the person overseeing the sale, passing a narrow stairway that led to the cellar. I found the woman in charge. "Whose house was this?" I asked. She knew me from my work at the *Oregonian* and apparently thought my question was rhetorical. She just nodded. "Sad story, huh." I still needed to hear her say it. "This was the house where . . . " Again, the nod. Then she said, "The family came through and took the big screen TV, the computers, the stuff worth money. They didn't want any of the art or personal things. My daughter is a psych student. She has Astrid's journals. There were some problems there. Things weren't what they seemed."

Having kept a journal since I was a teen, this last part horrified me. I would later call my cousin in Vegas and make her promise that if anything ever happened to me and Chan, she would get to the house and destroy my journals.

I wrote a check for ten dollars in a hand shaking so badly it was nearly illegible, and took the art to the car. How the hell was it that all these months later I would happen to be in Manzanita on the day they would hold the estate sale and just happen, after all those visits when I failed to drive by, to not only drive by in search of the house, but after eschewing estate sales for years, suddenly decide to stop by one? It was one of the eeriest things I've ever experienced.

I slipped in the front seat, sick in my stomach and all but hyperventilating.

Chan looked at me, and I could tell he was wondering, Oh hell, now what's the big drama?

"That's the house," I said.

He looked at me, frowning, pretending he didn't know what I was talking about, but he knew. He'd later admit he was just too creeped out to fully accept it yet. "You have to come inside with me," I said. "Just for a minute."

We walked in together, I couldn't explain it, but I needed to see the cellar. Later, a wise person suggested I was confronting Hunter. We walked down the old steps into a lower level filled with dishes and clothing, knick-knacks and, everywhere, the beautiful collages Schlaps made.

"Let's get out of here," I said. We drove in silence down the hill to Nehalem. I think we were both too stunned to say much.

I walked into the art gallery, where I found a tall woman with a headful of white-gray curls. "May I help you?" she asked.

"Are you Bonnie?"

"I am," she said, eyeing me curiously.

"I'm Lori Tobias with the *Oregonian*." Though the entire title was not likely necessary, I always said the whole six words, my tagline of sorts. My identity.

"Oh my God," she said, immediately reaching to hug me. When we parted, we were both in tears.

"Did you know this is the weekend of the estate sale?" I asked.

"I knew it was soon," she said. "I drove by and saw them getting it ready last week."

"Are you going to go?"

She shook her head. "I can't. I just can't do it."

"I'll go with you if you like," I said. "I was just there."

She shook her head, wiping at tears. I told her the next day was Chan's birthday. As it turned out, hers was that very day.

"You should have something of hers," I said. I told her about the piece I bought.

"I'll bet I know the piece," Bonnie said. "I framed that for her." Chan walked to the car and brought it inside. Bonnie gasped. "That's it. We worked so hard to get that done just right. It was a difficult piece because it is small."

"You should have it," I said. In truth, I didn't want to part with it, but it belonged to Bonnie.

"No," she said. "I couldn't."

"You must," I said. "It's your birthday, a gift from me." I pressed it into her trembling hands.

Bonnie called Richard and told him to hurry over to meet me. While we waited, we talked about the house, about the sale, about Schlaps's journals. Then Bonnie walked over to a display of art and pulled out a small piece of colorful flowers, a print of her work. "From me," she said. And then, "Wait, I have something else for you."

She opened a drawer and took out a piece framed similarly to the one I'd bought at the sale. "You have to have this."

In the picture taken at the wedding, Schlaps is waving triumphantly, her mouth open and you can almost hear the shout of joy.

"I can't take this," I said. I noticed Chan looked a little green.

"You must," Bonnie said. "I have another."

It was only when I looked down a second time that I saw that Hunter was also in the picture, sitting faded in the background, already a ghost.

After the deaths, Bonnie gave away the old family oak desk Hunter had given them and put the antique phonograph in storage.

"That was the most traumatic thing that ever happened to me," Bonnie told me recently. "I've lost parents, animals . . . that one was the biggest one for me. It hurt."

For years, despite all the evidence otherwise, Bonnie had a hard time accepting Hunter really did it—except for her memory of that last day.

"That is the only thing to me that puts it in the realm that he did it," she said. "I believe by the way he acted that evening with me that she was already dead. Something in my gut told me, I need to go see Astrid; I need to see Astrid. There was something that kept me from saying, 'Richard I need to go back to the house with you.' There was something horribly wrong. The way he kept backing away from me. The way he was so cold. He never behaved that way with me or anyone else."

That day he bought butter, cream, and cigarettes. Bonnie believes the dairy items were for the cats, which were locked inside.

"It was a big tall container of half and half. Why would you buy butter if you were going to kill yourself?

"When it gets right down to it, his behavior proves it to me. It's a good thing I did not go to the house. That would not have been pretty. He would have had to behave in the manner he did to keep me out of there just so I didn't do that, because I would have found her. I think he'd already done it.

"It is the oddest thing. I have a wedding picture of them, and Richard is fading. I have no explanation for it. But Astrid still has a presence in my life. She is still here."

I am naive about many things, but not politics. I learned politics from a Libertarian Alaska state representative in Juneau in 1986. Chan was headed for apprenticeship school. I didn't earn enough as a news reporter for the oldies AM station to cover the mortgage on our 630-square-foot log cabin. The Alaska Legislative Session had just gotten underway. I had applied for an opening with a Republican senator who represented the Kenai Peninsula. I didn't get the job and later learned it was due to my hair, which I'd recently colored burgundy, but I did get the idea of the jobs that might be out there. I picked up the phone and called every legislator from our area. Representative Andre Marrou returned my call, and within days I was bound for Juneau, with just enough money—Chan and I hoped—for the first month's rent on an apartment yet to be found, and no clue whatsoever about politics.

I was in for an education. I witnessed first-hand in those four months the lies, the backstabbing, the power grabs, the snobbery, the one-upmanship, the exclusion, the egos, the grandstanding that was the norm. Later, I would work two years in the Connecticut State Capital Press Corps, where I finally acknowledged I hated the whole business of politics. What on Earth was I doing focusing my career on it?

Now I was getting a fresh look at contemporary politics. The story began in August 2009, when the National Oceanic and Atmospheric Administration (NOAA) chose Newport to be the new home for its Pacific Fleet. Our small town was so happy, I wrote at the time, that I was surprised someone hadn't moved to strike up the band and lead an impromptu parade. The happiness, the surprise, the hope, the utter joy reverberated from one end of town to the other, Agate Beach to Nye, Nye Beach to the Bay Front, South Beach and on. Our little town had taken on the big dogs and, fair and square, absolutely above board, had won. The fleet had been homeported on Seattle's Lake Union for nearly fifty years, but the lease had run out and Newport had made the best offer.

I'd never thought Newport stood a chance to win the bid. Even when port manager Don Mann announced in 2008 that Newport was on the short list along with Bellingham, Port Angeles, and Lake Union, I sincerely believed we had no chance. The Port of Astoria had withdrawn its efforts for that very reason.

And yet, thanks largely to $19.5 million in lottery funds that allowed the port to set up a very attractive contract no one could match, we had done exactly that. The celebration in August 2009, as it turned out, was short lived.

From then on, it was two years of threats, intimidation, doubt, and ugly politics.

Even as Newport—all of Oregon, really—celebrated this amazing news, the state of Washington made it clear it would not let go of the homeport easily. US Senator Maria Cantwell of Washington fired the first round in a battle that showed politicians at their very worst. In a press release issued the same day the contract was awarded, Cantwell, the chairman of the subcommittee that oversees NOAA, wrote:

"I am extremely disappointed by NOAA's announcement today that it intends to relocate its Marine Operations Center to Newport, Oregon, and intend to fight it. For centuries, mariners have recognized the clear strategic and logistical benefits of housing ships in the Puget Sound. I seriously question whether relocating NOAA's ships outside of the Puget Sound is really the right move for NOAA. I'm also deeply concerned about the impact this decision will have on NOAA's employees and America's taxpayers, and that NOAA's scientific missions will suffer in the long run."

Three days later, the port signed the contract with NOAA and work began. Ten months later, the port was ready to break ground for construction of the center. It had been a harried rush of dredging and digging and all those other matters necessary to comply with state and federal permitting processes. The pile of sand from the dredging, dubbed locally Mt. NOAA, had added a new feature to the landscape and served as proof that work, and lots of it, was underway.

All the while, the Washington delegation kept up the efforts to stop the move to Newport. The Port of Bellingham protested the award, while legislators called for a review by the Government Accountability Office and Cantwell accused NOAA of withholding information and suggested "there may be even bigger problems that haven't yet come to light."

I, of course, was to remain unbiased, but how could I not cheer for our little town and not be repulsed by the ugliness of the politics? Some people take their losses gracefully. These were not those people.

The following summer, 444 people, including Oregon state legislators, congressmen, and their aides gathered under a tent to speechify, congratulate, and attempt to assure the audience that Washington would not wrest this honor from their hands. Obviously missing were the staff from NOAA, a glaring omission underscoring the fact this was not, in fact, a done deal. And despite all the backslapping and handshaking, just beneath the good cheer was a wariness, a wondering, what next and when?

As it happened, they didn't have to wait long. Two weeks later, Cantwell announced if the project went ahead her next step would be to call on Congress to halt funding.

Still, our little town continued to prevail. Then, six months from the day in August 2011 when at last it would dedicate the new NOAA Marine Operations Center, US Representative Jim McDermott of Washington introduced an amendment to the House spending bill to prevent NOAA from using its funding to pay for the costs of moving to Newport. US Representative Kurt Schrader of Oregon, took the floor and explained just what would happen if McDermott was successful, but the part that really hit home was the $50 million the government would lose in termination liabilities if NOAA did not honor its contract with the Port of Newport. The amendment failed 333 to 91.

On August 20, 2011, it was finally time to dedicate the new NOAA facility. It was a day of joy and congratulations, and yes, no small amount of relief. The sun was shining, the wind quiet. The $38 million project had come in on time and under budget. We were the little town that could and did. But after all the threats and efforts to thwart the bid, it was, in truth, fairly anticlimactic—and I doubt anyone minded a bit.

Politics was striking close to home, too. In September, the managing editor at the *Oregonian* called. I had already learned earlier that summer that the hope of going full-time—occasionally mentioned for several years, sometimes seemingly about to happen any moment—was not to be. Not only would I not gain hours, but I would lose some. All part-timers were being cut back to twenty-eight hours because of the Affordable Care Act. For the first time, I lost my Pollyannaish determination that things would get better.

There was nothing to do but keep finding the good stories, keep writing, keep my eye on that A1 centerpiece. And keep my fingers crossed. So on I charged.

That September, the US Life-Saving Service Heritage Association was hosting a tour of four former and current Coast Guard stations in Tilla-

Garibaldi's Pier's End is the longest of its kind in Oregon.

mook County. Two of the four buildings were old and private. Getting inside was a rare opportunity.

My first stop was the Barview station. Built in 1908, it was the only life-saving station from the Columbia River in Astoria to Yaquina Bay in Newport. It was the last US Life-Saving Service station built on the West Coast and the only one of its kind still in existence. The Historic Preservation League of Oregon listed it as one of the state's ten most endangered places.

I was eager to see it, but I arrived to find a much worn, faded old building, complete with a rather large black spider scaling the interior wall. Thieves had stolen the building's fine woodwork, light fixtures, and brass hinges, and a car that crashed and fell from Highway 101 above had flattened a second building. I feared it would be too difficult to photograph in any interesting way, and without good photos, stories were not likely to get good play. All I could see was the faded paint, the peeling walls, and random household items, like the old tub.

I was too busy to get in all of the four stations on one trip, so I made a second visit later. This time, the winds were gusting to sixty miles per hour and rain threatened to turn from drizzle to downpour at any moment. I met Port of Garibaldi manager Kevin Greenwood, planning to visit the aptly named Pier's End Boathouse. But when I saw the pier stretched out ahead of me—nearly two football fields long—I told Kevin I thought I could get an idea of what the place was like from where I stood. And surely, there were photos I could look at.

"No, you really need to see this for yourself," he said.

I could see the wood underfoot was slick with mildew and sea slime, the water below us churning with white caps. I said I really didn't have much time and could make do with what I had.

"It won't take long," he insisted.

I was out of excuses. And so, my raingear flapping in the wind, I began the slippery trek to the boathouse. Built in 1936 and ready for use in 1937, it came with its own marine railway to roll the boats into the water, and then, when the life-saving duties were done, to winch them back inside. It was a unique piece of history, and I was glad to have gotten a look inside, but mostly, I just wanted to get back across the great divide to the warmth and dryness of my car. As I walked and slipped my way back across the pier, waves breaking over it, I gripped the electrical conduit, wrapped in wire to deter birds, running its length. It was slow going and absolutely slicker than the proverbial snot. It was only when I crossed back to solid ground that I noted the blood on the cuff of my yellow raincoat. So tightly had I been gripping the rail, I'd cut my hand and never knew it.

My concerns about the photos of the US Life-Saving Service building, however, were unfounded. What I had seen as old and faded, in the eyes of photographer Beth Nakamura became a haunting tableau of shadows, light, and unexpected pops of color. Today, it seems unlikely that building will be saved, but the Pier's End Boathouse, originally named the US Coast Guard Lifeboat Station, is the subject of a major preservation effort and considered by local advocates a "national treasure."

Days later, we celebrated the seventy-fifth birthday of the Yaquina Bay Bridge, an occasion which included a pedestrian walkover—133 feet above the sea—and other festivities. I, of course, skipped the walkover. It was a well-attended community celebration, and I was happy to be a part of it, in my removed, reporter sort of way. But it was also the second time

Yaquina Bay Bridge.

I'd run into Dr. Steve Brown and not recognized him. I had no idea how sick he was, but I knew it couldn't be good.

In early October, Cody Myers, visiting for the Newport Jazz Festival, fell victim to David "Joey" Pedersen and Holly Grigsby, who had ties to white supremacist groups. The pair had already killed Pedersen's father and stepmother, and may have killed Myers because they believed he was Jewish. His body was found in the Mary's Peak area near Corvallis. He'd been shot in the head and chest. I didn't cover the story, which began when Myers was reported missing, and was handled from the Portland newsroom. Days later, the body of a fourth victim, Reginald Clark, fifty-three, of Eureka, California, was found. I learned about Clark, an African American man, through a tip from a Lincoln County sheriff's deputy and broke the story ahead of a scheduled press conference after confirming it through Eureka police.

But while reporters strive to be the first to break a story, there is no pleasure in reporting one like this. And this one felt much too close to home. The idea that Myers, a young, loving, happy person by all accounts, would come to Newport to take part in a music festival and die simply by virtue of having done so, cast a shadow of anger and sorrow over our little town. Life here, distant from more populated urban centers, generally felt safe, protected. But, of course, we were as vulnerable, as exposed, as anyone. Now when I ran to the Yaquina Head lighthouse mornings, about a three-mile roundtrip run that, particularly in the off season, was often deserted, I saw sinister motives in every car by the side of the road—no doubt pulled over for the view—and eventually I substituted a route in a more public area. And yet, Myers had encountered Pedersen and Grigsby by a public park, one generally filled with people walking their dogs, taking in the ocean view, enjoying the serenity of the coast.

Later that month came the story of a man who had looked at the soulless black eye of death and escaped only by the sheerest of luck. I learned of the attack through word of mouth, then met Bobby Gumm to hear his story.

After reading the surf report for the following morning, Gumm had traded shifts with another employee at the restaurant where he was a cook. He joined thirty or so other surfers in the waters off of South Beach State Park. The forty-one-year-old father of four was sitting on his surfboard when he felt something rub against his leg. Instinctively, he kicked at it and felt his foot connect with something he described as absolutely solid. He knew then this was no seal or sea lion but thought it might be a whale. But when he looked down, he saw a sixteen- to seventeen-foot great white shark rubbing against his legs. Witnesses on shore reported seeing the water churn, then a two-foot dorsal fin, followed by the great white erupting from the sea with a spray like a geyser. Gumm was thrown into the water when the shark took a chunk out of his surfboard. Terrified and uncertain if he'd actually survived or was experiencing the afterlife, Gumm prayed and paddled. Had he been prone on the board, as surfers often are, he would have been instantly decapitated.

Gumm was the second surfer I'd met who'd had a close encounter with a shark and survived. Two years earlier, I'd set out to cover the Nelscott Reef Big Wave Classic. My first stop was at a surf shop in Lincoln City to meet the competition's founder John Forse. Minutes into our conversation, Forse began lowering his jeans. Well, this is interesting, I thought. Then he directed my attention to the nasty scar on his exposed thigh where a great white had taken a bite as he surfed at Gleneden Beach in 1998. After sharing that story, Forse slipped off his shoe to show me his right foot, toeless after he ran over it with the lawn mower.

You can't make this stuff up.

Tillamook Sheriff Todd Anderson announced he was retiring by email. I was first surprised, then worried. Anderson loved his job. Was something wrong? Was he sick? No, he was just ready for a change, he said. Anderson had tipped me off to more stories than I could possibly count. I trusted him, and I counted on him. I feared his departure would leave a huge hole in my coverage of the vast Tillamook County.

The first time I worked with Anderson was when hunters found the bodies of pregnant Renee Morris and her three children in the Tillamook Forest just before Christmas in 2003. Each had been killed by Renee's husband, Edward Morris, who will spend the rest of his life in the state prison system for the murders. I worked with Anderson on the *Taki-Tooo* anniversary story and on a horrific sand rail accident that killed two and terribly injured several others. We worked together on fatal car crashes, capsizings, and search and rescues. Days after the news of his pending retirement, I drove up to his office, this time to write a profile of him. I'd been in his office maybe five minutes when he asked, "So, you want to go out and blow up some cars?" How do you say no to that?

His deputies were training with some FBI agents and Oregon State Troopers, and the training involved detonating bombs and then investigating the damage. Lucky me, I would get to detonate one, too. We drove off into the woods where I met a half a dozen or so men, all in law enforcement. I was the sole female in a forest of testosterone. It may have been serious work, but these boys were having a good time. Anderson got me a headset, showed me the car I'd be destroying, and then the bunch of us drove off to put some distance between the exploding car and ourselves. The law enforcement officials explained to me how it would go. Someone would give the signal, I'd yell "fire in the hole" three times, then push the button. Anderson offered to hold the device. I suggested someone else do the "fire in the hole" warning. Andy Long, the incoming sheriff, said he'd do the honors. He did and I pushed the button and felt the earth shake beneath my feet. I'd blown up my first—and, presumably last—car. It was

fun, it made my editor and my husband jealous, but it wasn't what I needed for a profile. So, a few weeks later, I headed north again, this time for
Anderson's official retirement party. It was there, nine years after the bodies of the Morris family were found, that I finally met Pat Elmore, mother
of Renee Morris, grandmother to the three murdered children. For years,
I'd asked Anderson to ask her to talk with me. She spoke at victims' meetings, but she wouldn't speak to the press. On this afternoon, Elmore was
the last one to stand up.

"He is like a brother to us," Elmore said. "He builds us up, and I hope
we build him up, also. He's my sheriff. He's my hero. One of the most
amazing things he did right away (after the murders), he came in and spent
the night in Hillsboro and drove to my house and picked me and another
witness up and drove us to Tillamook for the grand jury testimony. We
stopped and had lunch, and he drove us back home. Nobody had ever
heard of that. They said, 'Sheriffs don't do that.' I said, 'My sheriff does.
That's why I call him my sheriff.'

"He has been there at every level: personal and professional and private. Above and beyond, he cares. He really cares. He takes it personal as
far as he can. If he did that for every victim on the level he's done for me
I don't know how he's standing."

Elmore wiped a few tears; so did Anderson. And so did I, along with
most of the rest of the room.

NINE

SAND ON MY PILLOW, TEARS ON THE SAND

2012

The final shift for forty-seven employees at Tillamook Cheese Factory came on a Saturday in early February. The workers had gotten word that their jobs would be eliminated at the start of the New Year; the cheese cooperative would streamline its operation by moving jobs elsewhere and cutting unnecessary transportation costs. Many worried it was one more step by Tillamook County Creamery Association to move the operation out of Tillamook entirely. The jobs paid about sixteen dollars an hour, money that was nearly impossible to earn anywhere else nearby. I interviewed county commissioner Tim Josi, who learned about the layoffs from television news. He was angry and worried and said so, which got him in all kinds of hot water with his family, who still farmed and were members of the cheese cooperative.

I drove up to Tillamook the night before the workers' final day, and took a room in Oceanside in a little wood cabin facing the sea. It was going to be a hard story to do. When I'd first written about the impending job cuts in January, I'd reached out to everyone I could find who worked at the factory or knew someone who worked at the factory. I sent a message on a Facebook page the workers had created. I sent emails. I left phone messages. But not one person got back to me. Even the Teamster representative initially blew me off. When he finally did call, he made it clear he'd always felt the *Oregonian* was against the union. I told him I was the daughter of a Teamster and the wife of an IBEW (International Brotherhood of Electrical Workers) lineman, and he didn't have to worry about an anti-union bias from me, nor could he expect me to write against the cheese co-op. I'd do the story the way I tried to do every story: accurate and fair. We got along fine after that. But I also learned why no one would talk to me. Their severance package came with what some called a "gag order," a provision that they keep the package details confidential. You like to think if you were ever in the same boat you'd be the one to say, "Screw you." As I would learn soon enough, it's not that easy.

I drove over to the factory in the morning as workers arrived to begin their shift. I met Gail, a woman who asked that I not use her last name for fear she'd lose her severance. She and her coworkers cried as they hugged and signed a farewell card for their colleagues. I met a woman who had saved and saved for a house and finally secured the loan, only to lose it when news of the layoffs was announced.

In the afternoon, I returned with a photographer. We waited in the parking lot, envisioning a crowd of forty-seven workers bursting through the factory employee exit, but when quitting time came, the workers dribbled out only a few at a time. I was glad I'd taken the time to stop over that morning.

We would kill a little more time, and then I'd head back to the cabin to write. I pulled out my phone, thinking I'd call and check in with the Saturday editor and let her know what to expect. That's when I saw the email and the subject line: "Keiko's vet died." It took just an instant before it registered: Dr. Brown was dead.

I thought I should write the final story on Dr. Brown, but it was a Saturday. I had plenty of excuses why I couldn't. I was out of town, long out of hours, and I had no cell coverage at my room. But the truth was, I felt too close to the matter, too emotionally attached on many levels. And I knew to do the story I'd want to do I'd have to call the family, ask all the intrusive, nosey questions at a time when I expected they were already raw.

A week later at the memorial service—which must have been the best-attended service ever held in our little town—Larry, one of the vet techs, stopped me and asked why I hadn't written the obituary. I explained my reasons.

"Oh sure," he said. "But I got to tell you, when I read the piece by the other reporter, I said, 'That's not the house journalist.'"

We took our vacation once again that year in Belize and came home to all kinds of news. One day after we returned, I learned our editorial page editor had died of a heart attack. The story we ran said they found him in his car in the grocery store parking lot. I didn't know Bob Caldwell personally, but I knew he was well liked. I had spoken with him several times when he called to quiz me on some news story he was considering editorializing about. My editor wrote the obituary. But life soon got so crazy, I'd neglected to offer my condolences.

On the Monday after our vacation, I worked on yet another grim fishing story. There were six commercial fatalities in twenty-four hours—two in Curry County, four, twenty miles west of Wallapa Bay, as well as one grounding in Yaquina Bay, which saw four people and one dog rescued. As I wrote that story, the Umpqua Bank in Newport burned to the ground.

That afternoon, my editor called.

"I don't know if you heard about Bob Caldwell . . ."

"Oh, of course, I did and I am so sorry I didn't say anything," I said. "I meant to offer my condolences. I know you were all pretty close."

"Well," he said, "it turns out the story we reported wasn't quite true . . ."

The true story, uncovered by a reporter who took it upon himself to read the police report, was that Caldwell had not been sitting in his car in the grocery store parking lot, but at the home of a twenty-three-year-old student he paid for sex. It cost one of my editors her job, as she was the family friend who told the news desk the story about the grocery store. It's easy to say what she was did was wrong, but I've never had to choose between my dear friend and my job.

That evening, the worst snowstorm we'd experienced in twelve years on the coast began as we sat in the hot tub. Within hours, Cascade Head north of us on 101 was closed. The roof on our wood shed collapsed. Trees were falling everywhere. We listened to reports on the scanner of those panicked, unaccustomed to snow, calling 911 for help to get home. By midnight we'd lost power. Chan went to work. A short time later, I was awakened by a bizarre voice from the hall, warning "low calories, low calories." For a moment, I thought I must be losing my mind. Then I realized the phantom voice was the smoke alarm, now without electricity, warning "low batteries."

In the morning, I dressed in layers and headed out into the dark with my camera. I had taken only a few steps out of the driveway when I heard a loud crash. It wasn't until daylight that I saw the neighbor's tree had come down not twenty feet from where I'd been standing. Trees, their holds already tenuous in the sodden ground, toppled like twigs under the weight of the heavy snow, littering parks, highways, backyards, and parking lots everywhere. Chan called to say that Cape Foulweather was completely blocked. He was on his way to a PUD substation and grabbed a chainsaw to cut a path through the trees. Farther south in Coos County, traffic accident reports numbered over a hundred. By the time the snow stopped falling, Newport had received 6 inches, Tillamook, 8.5 and Florence, 5 inches. Most places, such accumulations would barely gain attention, but on the coast where the average yearly snowfall is two inches (and many years, not even so much as a dusting), it was more than enough to shut down our world. Schools, traffic, community events, city and county business all ground to a halt.

Emergency responders, powerlinemen, and others would deal with the storm damage for days, working to get the roads open and power back on in time for spring break. It's an important time here on the Oregon coast for all the tourists it brings at a time that is otherwise considered off-season, and we were lucky to have life back to normal by the time families pulled into town.

Spring break stories often fell to me. They were by their nature, positive stories, suggesting where families might go, what they might do. But I'd already written the obvious: Newport, Lincoln City, Seaside, Cannon Beach, Astoria. This time when my editors called, I suggested Manzanita. I was proud to be able to not only share my knowledge of the place, but convey some of its character, too. Never had such good intentions led to so much ugliness.

The story ran on A1, and at one point had won 286 "recommends" and held on as an "editor's pick" twenty-six hours after it posted. I was feeling so good that when I saw I had a voice message, I just assumed it would be more kudos. Instead, I found a woman ranting at me for sharing a place she apparently wanted only for herself. She ended with the conclusion, "You're probably dumb as hell." I wrote down her name and phone number and considered the message I'd leave for her. Not long after, I shredded it, fearing otherwise I would give in to the temptation to pick up the phone and sink to her level.

Later, I got a note, the first of many, from a man who wanted to know if someone had paid a fee to land the story on A1? And was I a stringer? He also wanted to know if I was working for certain people in Manzanita. I was not. In subsequent emails, he relayed a bit about the town's conflict between those who loved it and wanted it to remain unknown, and those who loved it and want to promote it. The latter, I am assuming, appreciate the economic growth and health tourism brings. As a visitor, I had been oblivious to the political infighting. The writer said I had damaged my integrity and the reputation of the *Oregonian*.

Years later, reading those emails still stung. Had I been that careless? Had I ruined Manzanita as he implied? I looked back over the story and found a feature about a little village in the shadow of better known coastal destinations, a little piece of oceanfront friendly to both families and dogs, where people, visitors, and locals, bike, hike, kayak, surf, or just enjoy the beauty all around. I wrote about the state park and Neahkahnie Mountain and the laid-back vibe that gives Manzanita its charm. Did I encourage people who'd never been there to visit? Probably. Did I ruin the town, I heartily hope not. Do I regret writing the piece? Absolutely not.

The big topic that summer was tsunami debris from Japan. When was it going to arrive? Had it already started? And what exactly could we expect? Would there be bodies or parts of bodies? Would the debris be big or little, of value, or dangerous? Contaminated with radiation or otherwise polluted? There was a lot of talk and speculation and very few concrete answers, except no, there probably would not be bodies—unless, of course an entire structure somehow made it intact with the deceased inside. Yes, for a time the conversation did get gruesome.

About fifteen months after the mega earthquake and ensuing tsunami struck Japan, I headed north at 6:00 a.m. to meet with a state park ranger and drive the stretch of beach from Seaside to Gearhart. He planned to show me debris already on the beach and to try to give me an idea how bad it was and how bad it might get. We met at 10:00 a.m. and headed to the nearest beach access. As we drove along, we stopped to pick up bigger pieces of litter: chunks of foam—the kind you might find stuffed in a cushion; plastic trash from foreign countries, including Finland, Mexico, and Germany; tires, bottles, rope, and fishing floats. And then there it was, a dead sea lion with a gaping wound in its head where the bullet had struck. It was the second in two days; there had been twenty since the month of April, the ranger said. I shot a couple of photos and finished the drive with the ranger. In the hotel room, I wrote a brief about the sea lions and sent the photos, but they were deemed too graphic and the story was buried inside the next day's paper. Months later, a woman called me sobbing about a sea lion that had been shot and was dying a slow, torturous death on the docks up by Astoria. She could find no one—not local authorities, not the sea life stranding operation, not the local vet or aquarium—to put it out of its misery. My editor and I decided it was time to do a piece on what was looking like the start of a mass murder, but another editor shot us down. We'd already done too many sea lion stories, she said. Rather than force a showdown, my editor and I agreed to give it a little time. I never did get to do that story.

In my hotel room that night, I got a start on my tsunami debris story, and wrote and filed a second piece about the Cannon Beach sandcastle building contest. By 1985, the contest had grown so popular it made national news and turned the little town of less than two thousand, one of Oregon's wealthiest, into a literal tourist trap of thirty thousand. Traffic was restricted to one way, and the only way out, at least the only reasonably quick way out, say in an emergency, was by helicopter. After that year, the publicity was toned way down, but now, nearly thirty years later, Cannon Beach was again hungry for visitors.

In the morning, I got in a fast walk on Seaside's promenade, then hurried for home. It was Chan's birthday, and I had plenty to do before he got home from work. As it turned out, getting ready for his birthday was the easy part. I pulled into Newport at about one in the afternoon and found a note from a friend in town asking me about the "monstrosity" that washed ashore on Agate Beach. Everyone assumed it was tsunami debris. Since that was the knee-jerk reaction to everything unusual on the beaches that year, my reaction was to pooh-pooh the whole thing. (I seem to have a habit of this and was once told by my editor that I was "notoriously difficult to impress" with stormy weather.) Besides, it couldn't be anything important. I had a birthday date with my hubs, and I'd already put in two, long full days, and it was only Tuesday. Then I heard back from Chris Havel at state parks. He wasn't commenting on whether or not it was from Japan, but he did confirm it was big, huge in fact: 66 feet long, 19 feet wide, and 7 feet tall. And there was a small plaque on the concrete mass written in Japanese. Shit. I grabbed my camera and drove the mile or so to Agate Beach, hoping the "monstrosity" was closer to the wayside than the Lucky Gap Trail, which was more convenient and closer to me, but which I avoided at all costs. It's the deal I struck with the snakes that like to sun themselves there and scare the crap out of me. I stayed off the trail; they stayed out of my yard.

So I parked at Agate Beach wayside and began slogging up and over the dunes, woefully aware as I trudged that I had worn the wrong shoes, which were now filling with sand. I had no choice but to take them off, and on I went. Finally, about fifteen sweaty, labored minutes later, I was close enough to get a fair shot with my zoom—saving me what I guessed would be at least another fifteen-minute trudge. I made the trek back to the car, grabbing my discarded shoes along the way, then hurried home to write

A March 2011 tsunami sent this dock across the Pacific, landing it on Newport's Agate Beach.

a short piece to go with the photo and, finally, got on with the birthday celebration. By morning, one of my colleagues at the *Oregonian* had confirmed through the Japanese consulate that it was indeed a dock ripped loose during the tsunami.

Day two, in pouring rain and temperatures more akin to November than June, I watched on Agate Beach, waterproof notepad in one hand, camera in the other, as teams from Oregon State University's Hatfield Marine Science Center scraped and torched living invasive species, including mussels, crabs, worms, barnacles, and kelp, from the dock. We all wore rain gear, the more sensible of us covered head to toe, but regardless we were all soaked. One man spoke to me as he worked, snot running relentless from his nose, no doubt undetectable by him from all the other moisture and goo associated with the rain, sand, and wind. I knew I must have looked like a drenched rat, but in some form or other, we all did. The scientists were happy to talk, but I was having a hard time getting it down. The pen simply would not work on the waterproof paper. Finally, someone pointed out the problem. I had forgotten that waterproof notepads work best with pencil.

Hours later, as I headed to the shower to warm up, I caught a glimpse in the mirror and saw mascara blackening both cheeks, my red nose, a testament to the unseasonable cold, and hair that hung in lank, dark clumps. My friend with the snot-leaking nose had nothing on me.

And so began the summer of the dock. It was a puzzle, a surprise, but more than anything, a worrisome warning. Foam inside the concrete provided flotation—that much was understood. But there were plenty of other questions: how had it floated all those thousands of miles undetected; how had all those millions of organisms that covered it not only survived but, given their numbers, thrived, and what the hell did all of this say for the future? Would there be more?

As the days passed, stories began coming from people who had spotted it. My husband saw it days earlier floating off of Depoe Bay, but unable to view its full size, assumed it was a local dock broken loose during high tide. At least three people called the Coast Guard to report seeing it bobbing in the surf, but right about the time the agency decided to look into it, another call came in for a search and rescue.

Despite the calls to save the 211-ton dock, including towing it around

An unknown artist gave the dock some color with a mural of the sea.

to the bay to replace the storm-damaged sea lion docks known as Bachelors' Row, it didn't take long for state parks to announce they would remove it, something one consultant suggested would be relatively easy. Meanwhile, visitors came by the thousands, overwhelming the police department, clogging the narrow, winding back road that leads to the wayside, and delighting local business owners who had suffered greatly during the recession. State parks tallied 14,833 visitors to Agate Beach Wayside during a week when they would normally see 2,000.

The visitors also stole or attempted to steal anything they could pry from the dock. Gone were two manhole inspection covers, one later returned, as well as "No Trespassing" and "Keep Off" signs hung by the state. When a parks ranger showed up to remove metal cleats, he encountered a passer-by with a toolbox about to do the same. One morning I arrived for my beach run to find some enterprising artist had even painted a small ocean scene on a beached corner.

I wrote at least seven stories in those early days. The first two alone produced somewhere in the vicinity of 300,000 hits on the *Oregonian*'s website. Throughout the summer, I'd update the story as plans were made and changed and finalized. There were still calls for the state to make the dock a permanent beach attraction. The wreck of the Peter Iredale, run aground in 1906, had been allowed to remain on the beach near Warrenton for more than a hundred years, and it remained a star attraction. So why not the dock? Just imagine, the state countered, what our beaches would look like in a hundred years if we continued to make washed up debris permanent features. And so, August 1 was set as the date to remove the dock with provisions to keep a large piece or two for memorial purposes.

Meanwhile, I worked on an interview with artist Rick Bartow, who was sculpting two twenty-foot poles to overlook the National Mall at the Smithsonian's National Museum of the American Indian. I did not know Bartow personally, though our paths had crossed at various times. The first came in my early days as a correspondent in 2004 when I had been out snooping around a South Beach neighborhood looking for information on Brandon Mayfield, who had been accused of a terrorist bombing in Madrid. Mayfield had once reportedly lived in the neighborhood across the bridge from Newport, and my editors sent me out to see what neighbors had to say about him. (The FBI later apologized to Mayfield, and paid his family a $2 million settlement.) No one was around that day in South Beach except for a man wearing hearing protection headphones and working with a weed whacker in an overgrown meadow. Maybe the only thing worse than walking up to someone cold and introducing yourself, is walking up behind that person when he can't hear a thing, has no idea you are there, who you are, or what you want. It is a good way to get yourself slugged or worse. And so I stood at some distance and hollered and waved my arms until finally he cut the weed whacker and said hello. He couldn't have been nicer or less startled at this strange woman standing in an open meadow carrying a camera and notepad.

Not only did he talk to me, he invited me inside the house that was part of his old family homestead, where I met his wife and child and was treated to a personal look at his art. He sent me home that day with a catalog of his work. In truth, I didn't know who Bartow was, but back in my office, I did my research, and came away impressed not only with his talent and renown, but first and foremost, his gracious and kind character.

Now he was trusting me to write about the Smithsonian project he called "the cherry on his lifetime cake." It was one of those rare times I carried a recorder, and I prayed it wouldn't let me down.

Bartow and I talked about a lot that day. How, when word came that the Smithsonian wanted the piece, he was just recovering from a stroke. There was no money upfront, and Bartow didn't have much himself, and he had no idea initially how he would make it happen. And yet, on "a lick and a promise," he was able to secure first a twenty-foot tree, and later, when more wood was required, a twelve-hundred-year-old tree and get it to Newport. Bartow, a member of the Wiyot Tribe of northern California, talked about Native American lore and its significance on the sculpture.

It was an honor to be there, an honor to be trusted to write the story, and I felt the weight of that. I wanted nothing so much as to get it right, to leave Bartow pleased he'd let me in. There was even talk that I might stop in DC on the way home to see my family in Pennsylvania for the September dedication of the sculpture, entitled, *We Were Always Here.*

Back in my office, I put in the earphones and went to work transcribing the audio. Over a few days, I crafted the thirty-inch story and filed it with my editors. I was happy with it, comfortable that I had captured the spirit of Bartow and his work. Then my editors figured out it was a commission, paid for with public money, and they wanted to know how much. Bartow asked me to please not publish the information. It was not a lot when all was said and done, but some people wouldn't understand, and he preferred to keep it private. I explained to my editor Bartow's position, explained that while I was a reporter, this was my home community, too, and it would be nice to be left with at least a few friends. But it was public money and thus, public information, and our readers had a right to know. In truth, I don't know if anyone else paid it much mind, but I did and I know Bartow did, too, and it's always been a shadow over the story, not because revealing the $200,000 commission was such a big deal, but because I could not escape the sense that I had betrayed a trust.

In the end, I didn't make that stop in DC. The *Oregonian* was looking at additional ways to cut costs and furloughs loomed ahead. Rick Bartow died in April 2016. I've always regretted that we hadn't sat down to talk just one more time.

As I prepared to write what would surely be among the last of my dock stories, I also began to make peace with the idea that my mom would not be with us for long. Her health had been steadily and somewhat mysteriously declining. She was drooling, and the doctors couldn't figure out why. She was losing five to six pounds a month because whole food was too hard to swallow, and she refused to eat it pureed. That my mother, who had battled her weight her whole life, was now too thin seemed just plain cruel. On top of it, she also had difficulty speaking. Yet there were no signs of a stroke. She had an appointment with the neurologist later that week.

That morning before I headed to the beach, I called the funeral home in Pennsylvania and asked if, when the time came, it would be possible to get a small urn for just some of the ashes. I'd never dealt with any cremains besides those belonging to my dogs, and I had no idea what was available. They said they'd email me an online catalog with keepsake urns, and I could choose from that. They'd keep the urn for me until it was needed. Something I thought was probably at least a few months away.

It was 7:30 a.m. when I headed to the beach. The demolition crew had laid a road of metal and wood across the sand for the trucks and crane to travel over, but it quickly became packed with pedestrians, happy not to have to trudge over those damned dunes. They came with their dogs and their kids, with picnic hampers, books, beach blankets, coolers, and cameras. I watched for a while, then came back to the office to file the first story, then went back to the beach. The wind was howling, and while the temperature was probably somewhere in the sixties, with the cold wind, it felt more like forty. I filed another late morning post by cell, not daring to leave for fear I'd never get another parking place. Finally, Randy Rasmussen, the photographer working on the story, and I walked to a nearby restaurant for lunch. It was a much-needed reprieve from the wind and sand, but too soon we were back out there.

The initial reports optimistically estimated the first cut—there were to be three—to be completed by early afternoon. Then, it was moved back a bit later and then, later still, until finally state parks spokesman Chris Havel quit giving estimates. And so I waited, enduring the relentless sandblasting by the wind. I whiled away the hours, talking with fellow reporters and photographers, checking in with my editors, and interviewing anyone of import who offered the shelter of a car. At 5:30 p.m., I finally walked back to my car and drove home. I didn't finish until eight that night, noting in my journal that I was "tired and everything hurt." The dock, despite a full day of efforts, remained stubbornly in place.

In the morning, my pillow was covered in sand. It was in my ears, in my hair, embedded in my skin. But the contractors planned an early start, and I was showered and on my way to the beach by 7:00 a.m. I was set to fly home soon, and my niece Tabby had emailed me to talk about what we might do during my stay. As I walked over the temporary road on the beach, I called and left her a message. The wind hadn't picked up yet, so I'd be able to hear her, I said. I watched the work get underway. The last I'd heard the workers had cut through the first section, but the force of the water kept it suctioned to the beach. I filed a quick brief to post on our website, then went to talk to Havel about plans and expectations for the day. The last thing I wanted to do was spend another day on the beach in the wind. My cell rang. It was Tabby, but I ignored it and continued my conversation with Havel. She rang in again, and I answered. She was crying. The nursing home had called. My mom was in hospice. Moments later, she called again, crying even harder. The home had called a second time and told her to get there right away.

I'd known ever since the shoulder surgery that my mom was dying. Until then, I would have given her another decade at least, but once she underwent the failed operation, it was clear there was only one direction she was headed, even with the temporary gains. But standing there and really trying to grasp that she would soon be gone, might even be gone already, did not even seem possible. And I had no idea what to do. I froze. I think I may have told one of the other reporters hanging around. I may have called my husband. Finally, I asked Havel for a ride to my car. I thought I would head home, pick up Mugsy, and go for an iced coffee. I guess I was just trying to give myself something concrete to do. I walked into the office and called Tabby, who sobbed, "I didn't make it on time." My mom died at 10:55 a.m. Eastern Daylight Time—about the same time I was asking Havel for a ride. I called my cousin, who made me repeat the news several times. I called my brother, who would himself be gone in little more than a year. I called the newsroom, fighting to form the words, struggling not to break down. I called nieces and nephews, childhood friends.

And in the middle of it all, I planned the funeral with my niece. I have no idea what else I did that day, except that when I finally noted the time, it was 2:00 p.m. That afternoon, when I opened my email, I saw that the order of emails in my saved box had been reversed—rather than newest to oldest, the oldest was now on top. It was a card just to say, "I love you," sent from my mom two years before. The link no longer worked, but I understood the message just the same.

Thirteen days later, Chan and I spent the afternoon at the casino to celebrate my birthday. Celebrate is hardly the right word. Something about my birthday and the loss of my mother combined left me feeling completely untethered. But we made the effort. Afterward, when we pulled into the driveway, I saw a box on the front porch. It could have been anything. It was, after all, my birthday, and I order my share from the Internet. But I knew. Although I'd completed the order only days earlier, I knew.

"Oh no," I said. "Don't tell me . . ."

"What?" Chan asked, slightly panicked.

"That box, my mom . . ."

And sure enough, there beside the flowers from a friend, were my mom's cremains.

Three plus years had passed since my story on the renewed efforts to solve the cold murder cases of Jennifer Esson and Kara Leas, with no breaks so far as I knew. Then, in early September, as I backed out of Fred Meyer's parking lot, my cell phone rang. It was Lincoln County District Attorney Rob Bovett. A story, a big story, was about to break, and he wanted me to be ready. The conversation was off the record, and he would tell me only enough to make sure I understood the import. Someone with local ties had been linked by DNA to a cold case murder in British Columbia. The Royal Mounted Police planned a press conference in late September.

It was going to be big, and he was going to help me break it.

About a week before the press conference, Bovett and detective Ron Benson met with me—again off the record—to share details of what was about to happen so I would be ready to write and file as soon as the press conference was held. A prison inmate, who had been arrested in Newport in 1995 after attempting to rape and threatening to kill a woman, had been linked to the murder of Colleen MacMillen, a sixteen-year-old girl who disappeared in 1974 near Lac La Hache, British Columbia. She was last seen alive on Highway 97 and found murdered off a logging road about twenty-nine miles away. Detectives matched DNA found on MacMillen to Bobby Jack Fowler, who had died at the Snake River Correctional Institution in 2006 while serving time for his crime in Oregon. The victim had saved herself by jumping naked from a second-floor motel room window. The Canadian police believed Fowler could be linked to at least nine other murders going back to 1969 on the stretch of road known as the Highway of Tears. It was big news for the Canadians and for us. Bovett and Benson believed Fowler may have murdered Jennifer Esson and Kara Leas.

The press conference was set for the morning of September 25. At my editor's urging, I wrote the story a day ahead of time so that once the press conference got underway we could post it. I'd been sitting on the story for nearly three weeks and was ready to go.

That night at about six, I saw an inhouse email from a colleague in Portland asking if anyone knew anything about a press conference in Canada involving an Oregon inmate. My heart hit the floor. Then, one of my editors called to say a reporter had called the newsroom and asked what they knew. Someone had leaked the story. Someone else was going to break it. There was no way I could let that happen. I called my editor at home and the night editor on the city desk, and we raced to edit my story and get it posted and ready for print before the deadline. We made the latter by a hair. Then a reporter called from Canada. His competition was all over the story and he needed help finding a source. I shared Rob Bovett's information with him and told him where to find my story and then—and I still can't believe I was quite so direct, but I was—I said, "If you fuck with me—if you plagiarize my story—I will find you, and you will pay."

My phone started ringing at six in the morning. By midafternoon, I'd done three radio interviews and one for television. A former Toronto foreign correspondent, who I'd met while traveling in Switzerland, wrote in an email, "You are a celebrity here." But I also learned that I'd made a mistake, calling it the Trail of Tears, when, in fact, it is the Highway of Tears.

For a time, a connection to Fowler in the cold case looked hopeful. There was a police report that put his car north of Newport right about the same time the girls disappeared, but it led to nothing. Later, it was revealed that there was solid evidence that Fowler was far away from Newport just days before the murders and couldn't have possibly made it here by the day the girls disappeared. But there was also talk of an accomplice. In any case, if Fowler was the killer, he's taken that secret to the grave.

There was no doubt times were changing. From the first story I wrote for the *Oregonian*, even before I was a correspondent and still freelancing, the editors and copy editors were diligent to a fault about their job. And, as annoying as the multiple phone calls could be when a story was about to run, I was beginning to understand just how lucky I'd been that they had had my back. When the mistakes did make it through, usually they were small, stupid things that most people didn't notice. But the one that will forever stand out as beyond stupid came in my last story of the year. It was one of those win-win, feel good stories, just the kind editors like to see around the holidays when things can get pretty quiet. The state, a couple of small communities, and a nonprofit environmental group had teamed up to reduce flooding on a highway near Seaside. They would do so by removing a structure built forty plus years prior that was intended to keep the water off a farmer's field. Instead, it pushed water up onto the highway, often necessitating its closure during the wettest days of the year. The story ran on the metro cover. The phone started ringing early, my email filled, and I turned a few shades of red. As one woman politely wrote: "Perhaps you may have a different dictionary than I, but mine defines the word 'levy'—an imposing and collecting of a tax, or simply a tax. Maybe you meant 'levee'—"

TEN

EXCITING PLANS

2013

I had my own reasons for wanting to write about Gail Hand's efforts in Seaside, Oregon, to help Seaside Heights, New Jersey, rebuild after Hurricane Sandy. In 1970, the summer I would turn ten, my parents took me and my sister, Penny, to the shore for the first time, and we went to Seaside Heights. A handful of relatives came with us. We stayed in motel rooms and spent our days on the beach or walking the boardwalk. And on one of those walks, we came to the bumper cars.

No one ever called me a daddy's girl. My dad worked long, hard hours, rising early in the morning to drive to work, then driving a truck around central Pennsylvania all day, and sometimes, if overtime was available, into the evening. He'd arrive home, eat his dinner at the table with a quart of beer and his newspaper, and shortly after go to bed. The next day it was time to start all over again. I adored my dad and worked hard to please him. I was a tomboy. Actually, I was a wannabe tomboy, who made a great effort to portray a toughness that was not real. I learned to mow our very large yard to impress my dad. I polished his boots and ironed his handkerchiefs.

If there was ever a place where I wanted to excel beneath my father's watchful eyes, it was in one of those colorful, miniature cars in Seaside Heights. After all, he had been a racecar driver. His brother was one of the best-known drivers on the East Coast. He had friends who raced, and we never missed watching the Indy.

They bought my ticket, and I climbed in. I put the pedal to the floor and began to spin. I tried everything, braking, turning the wheel, but all I did was spin in that one little circle, making me the perfect target for every other kid, all boys as far as I could see, on the ride. It was all I could do not to burst into tears, and I must have looked it. I sneaked a glance at my father, who offered me an encouraging smile. About the time I got the damned thing stopped and made forward progress, time was up. Later, I heard my dad tell mom he thought he'd laugh until he cried.

After my dad died in 2005, we booked a room in Seaside, the Oregon coast town most like East Coast shore towns, and I bought tickets for the bumper cars. I can't say I was much better at it then, though I did get in some good hits. But this time when the tears threatened, I let them fall.

And so in the spring of 2012, when Gail Handy organized a weekend of fun in Seaside to raise money for people in Seaside Heights, I agreed to do a story. I called Seaside Heights Mayor Bill Akers and talked to a couple of community booster types. Seaside Heights, it turns out, is not so different from Seaside or most other Oregon coast towns. There is a high level of poverty, many school kids are on reduced or free lunches. There are few good paying jobs, and the off season—which is the bulk of the year—makes charity crucial to the survival of many families. I had a good time sharing my history of Seaside Heights with Mayor Akers, and by the time we hung up, I'd agreed to visit on my next trip home. "We'll welcome you with open arms," he said. We planned the trip for late September and figured we'd spend two nights in a hotel along the newly built boardwalk.

It wasn't just a goodwill trip down a childhood memory lane, but a chance to share it with my husband and perhaps even do a story on the new sign at the entrance to town that the donations from Seaside, Oregon, had helped buy.

Then, in mid-September, I turned on the TV and watched the Jersey shore burn. An electrical fire devastated blocks of the boardwalk in Seaside Park and Seaside Heights. The six-alarm fire was later determined to have been caused by wire that had been submerged during Hurricane Sandy. Two weeks later, we flew back East. But I just didn't have the heart to visit the newly ravaged Seaside Heights.

When Kathy Wagner called me in late 2012, her tale didn't seem quite plausible. I had no reason to doubt her integrity; I just questioned if perhaps she had her facts straight. Her niece had been brutally assaulted by a man who had once been her boyfriend. The court case was set for November, but victim April Loper, thirty-four, had died in a car crash with her father, Daniel Loper, in October on Highway 20. Now it seemed the accused, Thomas Acosta, fifty-one, might very well go free on charges that included first-degree sodomy, two counts of first-degree unlawful sexual penetration, first-degree rape, three counts of second-degree sexual abuse, coercion, two counts of strangulation, three counts of fourth-degree assault, menacing, and unlawful use of a weapon.

Loper had given her testimony to police, told her story to the nurse who conducted the medical exam, and worked hard with the district attorney's office to ensure they would be ready when her day in court came. But when Loper died, almost all of the testimony became inadmissible and was deemed instead hearsay.

Loper and Acosta began dating in October 2011. It's probably a good bet she didn't know his history, which included accusations of sexually assaulting and repeatedly raping a former girlfriend in Washington, assaulting and threatening to kill a former girlfriend in Texas, and sexually assaulting a male acquaintance in California. It didn't take her long to figure out she'd signed on with the wrong beau. The young woman who loved nature, music, and people soon grew quiet and fearful. She wanted to end it with Acosta but was afraid to. Then on December 15, while they worked at her thrift store in Aquarium Village in South Beach, Acosta attacked her. When Loper struck him back, he knocked her unconscious. She awoke in the loft of the shop, bound with electrical tape. Throughout the night, Acosta repeatedly assaulted, sodomized, and raped Loper.

After he freed her in the morning, Loper confided in friends, but swore them to secrecy, fearful he would make good on his threats to hurt her family or her dog. On Christmas Eve, he showed up in his van and Loper left with him, again hoping to protect her family. Acosta drove her to Redding, California, where the rape, assault, and threats continued. Loper managed to escape on New Year's Day 2012. Acosta was arrested several weeks later and had been in the Lincoln County jail since.

But there was another part to the story—one I didn't expand on for the *Oregonian*, though it seemed everyone read between the lines and put the pieces together. Also in the car crash with Loper and her father was Loper's two-month-old son. For years, Loper had tried and failed to get pregnant and believed it wasn't a possibility. In the summer of 2012, she realized her dream of bearing a child. Only the baby survived the crash.

Now it seemed there was a very good chance that Acosta might walk. Not only would he be a free man, but if the child was his, what rights would he have to him?

Wagner hoped if I told Loper's story, the public reaction might persuade the powers that be to go forward with the prosecution. Whether the media attention had anything to do with it or not, the case did move forward. In February, as Acosta, an ugly, bald little man, sat handcuffed up front in his orange jumpsuit, jurors listened through eight days of testimony. But they heard only a fraction of what prosecutors had gathered, with the defense objecting frequently and the judge usually sustaining the objections. It's wasn't like on TV where the judge instructs the jury to ignore evidence they shouldn't have heard. In this case, the jurors were sent from the room over and over and over again, then called back, only to be sent out yet again.

The media was well represented with reporters from the local paper, a website, and radio station. Dave Morgan is the founder, reporter, photographer, videographer, and wears every other hat associated with the News Lincoln County website. It is a well-read blog, and over the years Morgan has worked his ass off to make sure he is always on top of breaking news.

One day in the courtroom, Judge Thomas Branford directed Morgan, who'd been standing with his camera, to take a seat. Morgan did, but later stood again with his camera. Branford called a recess, and I walked over to Morgan and asked if he wasn't supposed to be sitting? No, he said. He thought the judge meant only when the jurors were coming and going. Seconds later, a deputy came inside and physically removed Morgan. He was banned from the courthouse, and despite a letter explaining his bad hearing, as well as an apology, the ban held, and Morgan was left to wait outside, depending on the rest of us to fill him in on what was happening inside the courtroom.

Meanwhile, my editor forwarded a letter sent to me at the *Oregonian*'s Portland address. It was from Acosta, decorated in crayon with Disney characters. From what I could tell, it was bits and pieces of court documents and some disjointed attempt that made little sense to proclaim his innocence. He obviously had no idea I was sitting in the courtroom watching him each day.

Finally, after eight days of testimony, the case began winding down. It was a Friday, typically a day I didn't work as I was out of hours by the end of the week. I expected the case to go to the jury sometime later that afternoon, and I figured we might not hear a verdict until after the weekend. So I had plenty of time, I thought. I went to the gym, came home, and showered. I was soaked and still in my robe when my cell phone beeped, and I found Kathy Wagner on the other end with news that I'd better get to the courthouse fast. Panicked I was about to miss something big, I half dried my hair, threw on some makeup and clothing, and raced to the courthouse. As it turned out, the judge was just giving jurors their instructions.

And so the wait began.

The jury took less than four hours to come back with the verdict: guilty of first-degree sodomy, second-degree sexual abuse, and two counts of second-degree assault. There may not have been much admissible evidence, but eyewitness accounts from friends and family who saw Loper's black eye, her swollen face, the various cuts and bruises and marks around her wrists, as well as testimony from a nurse and police reports, were enough.

Six days later, Loper's mother and sister faced Acosta in the courtroom, blasting him with their anger. Acosta laughed and winked at them. The judge sentenced Acosta to eight years and four months in state prison.

A couple of scares hit a little too close that spring. One I simply could not objectively write about; the other wasn't necessarily newsworthy, and I was hoping it would stay that way.

Subcontractors working for the PUD were setting a tower with a crane in Alsea Bay. My husband, now the line supervisor, had just got in the door at the end of his workday when his cell rang. His face went white as he repeated what he'd just heard, "Crane and tower in Alsea Bay. Oh my God." With little explanation, he was out the door. I picked up the phone and called the newsroom.

"I'm going to tell you right now, I can't cover this, but you better get someone on the phone with the PUD . . ." In the end, no one was hurt, but long before I knew that, I knew it was one of those rare times I absolutely could not claim to be unbiased.

That same spring, I got a request to connect with a man on LinkedIn. His profile listed him as an editor at the *Oregonian*. I didn't recognize the name, Daniel Crawford, but there were lots of editors I didn't know, and he mentioned that he'd just started in January. I never gave it a second thought, especially with the staff in such constant flux.

I clicked the link to connect, and soon got a note back, thanking me. He said it was good to be linked to a contemporary, "Plus you have a wonderful face." Okay, I thought, that was weird, but . . ." Then he wrote to ask at what age I knew I wanted to write? I responded, fourteen. I am always game to talk about writing, and so I didn't think that much of it. I figured since it was the weekend, he was having a slow day. We had a short "chat." I told him I worked from a home office, but that one of these days when I got into the newsroom, perhaps we would meet.

On Monday, I mentioned the interaction to one of my colleagues on the breaking news team. She told me to hang on, then came back on to say she'd checked the newsroom roster and no such person existed. About then, my editor arrived. Daniel Crawford had nothing, of course, to do with the *Oregonian*. One of our managing editors contacted LinkedIn, but it was days before she got a reply. I never heard another word from Crawford—if that was really his name.

Ten years had passed since the *Taki-Tooo* crashed on the Tillamook Bay bar, taking the lives of eleven sports fishermen out to enjoy Father's Day. Once more, it fell to me to write the anniversary story. Tamara Buell Mautner, the deckhand who no doubt helped save peoples' lives by yelling at them to get out of their raingear, now owned the fishing charter and was a captain herself. She didn't want to meet to talk about it again but was willing to answer some questions by email. She was married, the mother of two, and preferred to spend the bulk of her time mothering. Once again, I picked up the phone and called Mark Hamlett. We talked about the decade that had passed, and then I called his son-in-law, Brian Loll, who lost his own dad, Edward Loll. He'd made some peace with the loss and had forgiven all involved. But he still watched the tragedy unfold in his head like an endlessly looping video.

A few months later, I got a call from Mark. He and his wife Judy were coming to the coast to celebrate their anniversary and wondered if we might get together. After nine years of talking on the phone, I finally met the couple at a little restaurant on the Bayfront, and we shared our stories of the Oregon coast. Mark had helped build the Inn at Otter Rock, his start in the construction business. And we talked about the *Taki-Tooo* a lot. Mark believes a higher power saved his son, Daniel. Daniel was on the deck when the *Taki-Tooo* rolled. One of the eyewitnesses on the beach saw the boat roll twice. He saw a young man holding on, but by the second roll he was gone. Daniel recalled being in the water, seeing the bodies floating around him and then a life raft. He swam for the life raft. An instant later he was hitting his head on the stairs inside the boat. No one could explain how he'd been outside, then back inside.

When asked, Mark likes to say, "Angels work for me."

Over lunch that afternoon Mark told me how he'd walked the beach looking for his family. He found his sons, but couldn't find his son-in-law, Brian. He waited for police to bring Brian's father's body ashore and identified him, then caught a ride to the hospital. He walked through the front door in borrowed sweat pants, wrapped in a blanket. Everyone else had gone through the ER entrance and now hospital staff tried stopping him, but Mark wouldn't be stopped. Although he'd seen his sons on the beach, he didn't know for certain how they were. Then he heard their voices and knew the three were alive.

The June 2013 memo began: "Dear colleagues: Today we are unveiling exciting plans for the future of our company . . ."

Those exciting plans included the layoffs of thirty-five reporters, photographers, and editors—some whose jobs were posted within days, some who were hired back, and a few who asked to be let go. I spent very little time at the *Oregonian* offices but knew from conversations with colleagues that spirits were about as low as they could go. I heard about the "exciting plans" via the Internet. My editor called to update me a short time later. And still I thought I was safe—or at least as safe as anyone. After all, I reasoned, as I had so many other times before, I was a cheap date, offering the paper free office space, and I knew the coast better than anyone; I had sources in every nook and cranny over 360-odd miles.

I worked my tail off. I broke important stories and . . . They knew my worth. Didn't they?

We were to hear our fate by day's end. But day's end came and went, and I still knew nothing and still hoped that meant something good. A former reporter set up a fund to pay the bar tab at Higgins in Portland. By evening, it had grown to $3,000. I sat home in Newport and drank alone.

In the morning, I checked out my page one story on the Face Rock Creamery. I thought surely, A1 centerpiece had to mean something. I went to the gym feeling maybe a tad reassured, and came home expecting to see a message. But there was none. Then I started hearing the names of those who would be leaving, and I knew if they were gone, how could I possibly be safe? I couldn't wait any longer. I called the managing editor. He said he was just picking up the phone to call, which almost allowed me to think . . . and then he said, "I'm sorry, the news is not good." He said what a quality journalist I was and how much he respected and liked me as a person. I said thanks. I was trying to be the big person, trying to keep my chin up and walk away with my pride and dignity intact. I had about nine weeks before it would be over, and I received my last check with severance pay. I said I understood. But I didn't.

ELEVEN

A BOOK IN THIS BEAT

Almost from the start, I knew there was a book in this beat—the strange coincidences, the way stories had seemed to find me, the unlikely friendships I'd forged. And so, from the day I learned I would lose my job, I had a mission.

One by one, I read through all of my old journals, starting from the year I signed on as a correspondent. I flipped through the dozens and dozens of slender white reporter's notebooks I'd kept over the years, and I cataloged all the news stories that had stayed with me, and stumbled, as well, on a few that had not.

And I wrote, working every day from my laptop in front of the woodstove. I see now it was my therapy of adjusting to the new reality, of now being simply Lori Tobias without the tag phrase, "I write for the *Oregonian.*"

I was giving myself hope. I was telling myself it was not the end, but the future, that I could remain relevant. But on my own again, it felt exactly like the end. Who would I write for? Who would I go to when the big story broke? What was I going to do? My novel, written in the stolen hours between breaking news stories, was finished and had been rejected so many times I'd lost count. I had all but given up on agents after one wrote to say she loved the story, but hated the character around whom the whole plot revolved. "Could I get rid of him? And did such people really even exist in Alaska?"

But being unemployed was not without an upside. I could once again call my days my own. I could speak my mind, finally, about politics. I could look at my computer, answer my phone any time, without fearing I would have to go to work. I could go out and be part of the community.

I began pursuing freelance work again, something I started doing back in 1989 when I wrote the then shocking tale of a Connecticut woman I'd met through the Hemlock Society. She planned to commit suicide when her cancer advanced. I started writing a small column for a coastal tourism newspaper that paid just enough to buy a good bottle or two of wine each month, and in time, I was writing for the *Oregonian* again. But freelancing is not what it used to be. When I arrived on the coast in the fall of 2000, I was paid $1.50 a word to write for one home magazine and $800 a feature for another. Now, with blogs and aggregates and the dying market of print, I was offered pennies. I corresponded with a guy in Texas for days who was looking for a writer, but whenever the issue of money came up, he would say only that the pay would be appropriate. When we finally talked on the phone, he told me I would need to sign on to Skype when I started writing so he could make sure I was doing what I was supposed to be doing, and for this he would pay me two cents a word. I hooted out loud and hung up.

Once, after months of talking story ideas with the West Coast editor at one of the biggest dailies in this country, I finally worked up the pitch he'd requested. He responded that he'd just learned he was to be laid off, too.

Nearly my entire life had been about writing, but it seemed the written word no longer held much value. The bright spots were far and few between.

And then an amazing thing happened.

On a sunny afternoon, as I was hard at it on my laptop, the phone rang. It was a 907 area code—Alaska, which probably meant someone in Chan's family or, perhaps, a friend. I picked up.

"Hi Lori," she said. "This is Peggy, you sent me your novel."

"Yes," I said, barely able to breathe.

"I love it," she said.

And so it was that dream with the slimmest chance of coming true, did.

It took like what seemed forever, but in due time *Wander* was published. My first reading was at Ray Shackelford's Nehalem Bay Winery, where I began learning to overcome my stage fright. No easy task, I assure you. That day, Ray picked me up at the nearby motel and chauffeured me to the winery where the profile I wrote all those years ago still hangs framed in the tasting room. Ray ordered thirteen books to be signed for various family members; we posed together for photos and once again, a professional source became a friend. Likewise, Dave Dillon, my source for news tips on the north coast, appointed himself my patron and secured me a reading at the prestigious Hoffman Center for the Arts.

Months later, I read in New York. New York! When I finished, I joined my niece and friends outside as they headed out for a night on the town. A young man approached. "Are you Lori Tobias?" he asked. Turns out he was from the Oregon coast, too. He'd read my *Oregon Coast Today* column about my upcoming trip to the city and just happened to be visiting there himself. Small world indeed.

From New York, I returned to central Pennsylvania to read to the hometown crowd in Hershey and later to a room packed with colleagues, old neighbors, and friends at the Tattered Cover in Denver, and to my friends and family at the Barnes and Noble in Anchorage. I signed and read up and down the Oregon coast, made new friends and revived old friendships. *Wander* would go on to win the Nancy Pearl Book Award and be named as a finalist in the International Book Awards, and it was every bit as amazing as I'd dreamed.

Meantime, I still had to earn a living. But oddly, I found the taste I'd acquired for the rush of a developing story, the race to break the news, was dying. I suspected my reporting days were done. I had by then lost my mother, my job and, in December 2013, my only brother. All in only two years and eight months. It wasn't that I didn't care about the stories going on around me anymore, but maybe that I cared too much. The shields of the trade—the notebook, pen, camera—were no longer sufficient buffers; the front page, leading posts, no longer adequate rewards.

It hit home for me on November 3, the day my father would have turned eighty-five. That was the evening I sat down at my computer and read the news that Jillian McCabe had thrown her six-year-old autistic son, London McCabe, off of the Yaquina Bay Bridge, a drop of 133 feet. As I read it, I heard myself say out loud, "Oh God, no." There was a time I would have had the phone in hand before I even finished reading the news. Because that was my job. But on that night, I called no one. I didn't even send an email.

I knew the story needed to be told, but I just didn't have the heart to rush out into the night, notebook in hand, camera slung over my shoulder, to ask the questions that had to be asked of the only people who could answer them.

In the morning, I found a text from an *Oregonian* editor sent just before midnight, asking me to call the news desk. I said I was busy. But I couldn't shake the story.

Weeks later on an afternoon after the memorial service for London had passed, after the flowers, balloons, and stuffed animals had been cleared from the bridge and then more cleared again, I sent a note to London's father, Matt McCabe. I had learned over the years that as hard as those calls are to make, as difficult as it is to knock on those doors, frequently people want to talk about the person they lost. They want the world to know why that person was special, loved, and now mourned. And so, when Matt wrote back to me, I told him if he ever wanted to tell the world about his beautiful blue-eyed, golden-haired boy, I'd be honored to write it.

The story Matt wanted to share was of a boy who brought joy and love into his and many others' lives. He wanted the world to know, too, that just because someone has a disability, it does not disqualify them from getting to live the life they deserve to live.

We sat down together at a local restaurant a few days before Father's Day—the first since Matt had lost his son. Sitting across the table from me, he described the son who loved to jump and cuddle, who was tender hearted and just beginning to use words. The last words London ever said to him were "bye-bye."

My conversation with Matt will always stay with me. London loved hats, and when I sat down across from Matt, he was also wearing a hat, a new tradition he had started in honor of his boy.

"Parents don't move on," he told me. "There is never closure. It may not be something they talk about, but it's something they feel every minute of every day. And that's why I'll always be a father. Because I'll always have the memories and the loss."

A few mornings after the story ran in the *Oregonian*, I found a note in my email from Mark Hamlett:

Lori, I have to commend you on your recent article about a father's loss of a challenged 6 year old. You are able to feel the edge of life and expose it to those who will see your effort. I worked on the Embarcadero for almost two years. I watched the storms come and go and the fog transform The Yaquina Bridge from an eerie skeleton to an elegant imposing structure. It is hard to think of that little guy's walk up that arch, knowing how close I came to having none of my grandchildren. I am so very grateful to have them around. Thanks for your sensitivity with our story as well. Mark and Judy and the troops.

No words could have better exemplified what I love most about being a journalist: the people I meet, the absolute trust they put in me to tell their story and to get it right.

I thought for a time I was done being a journalist. Now it seems I was merely catching my breath. Oh, I often try to resist the call of a break-ing story, but often as not, when called, I just can't say no. Those stories are frequently tragic: the motel fire that killed four, ignited after a woman dropped a cigarette in bed; the capsizing of the F/V *Mary B II*. Three men died, including local Joshua Porter, who'd told friends the trip would be his last. He wasn't comfortable with the inexperience of the East Coast skipper and crewmate.

It bares noting that this particular tragedy occurred as the US Coast Guard struggled to help fishermen caught up in fast-building seas that grew from a nearly flat four feet to twenty feet, imperiling the most experi-enced of mariners. They did so during the thirty-five-day federal govern-ment shut down, working without pay, at the mercy of donations from the community to feed themselves and their families. Life here on the edge of the Pacific would be unimaginable without the Coast Guard, and my hat is off to them every single day.

Not all stories that land on my desk are tragic. Occasionally they are fun, enlightening, or shine a spotlight on some lovely bit of the Oregon coast. One recent story told the tale of a person whose life was rooted in sorrow, shame, and longing, and then, through what seemed an enormous act of courage, transformed into one triumphant and proud.

The Newport Fishermen's Memorial Sanctuary is located at the Yaquina Bay State Park and dedicated to Lincoln County based fishermen lost at sea since 1900.

When Claire E. Hall invited me to lunch in early 2018, the world still knew her as him—Bill Hall, four-term Lincoln county commissioner, former journalist, advocate for the homeless and author of *McCallandia*. Hall often sought me out, sometimes with a tip about a news story he thought needed coverage, sometimes just to talk writing. I assumed on that January day he had a story for me, perhaps on his efforts toward affordable housing, perhaps on some behind-the-scenes dealing that needed revealed. I was not even remotely close.

Hall was planning to transition from male to female, and he wanted me to be the one to share his—soon-to-be her—story. I was honored and agreed to accompany him on the journey for a story for the *Oregonian*. But I was also worried for Hall. I worried about the public humiliation, cruelty, violence even, that would surely follow.

I have no doubt she's experienced it all. Her stepchildren sent word she was never to contact them; her ex quit speaking to her. Nonetheless, Hall has transitioned with the utmost dignity, lending her voice to the support and education of others. Hall's story continues. She writes an advice blog, "Ask Claire," and talks of the possibilities for her future: A run for governor? A book? Life on a larger stage? When that story breaks, I'd be happy to be the one to share it.

And so the stories go.

The world of writing, of books and newspapers, of how we read and where we read, is changing, changing so fast it's hard to imagine what exactly we'll be left with. But we will always have our stories, of that much I am sure. And that I am able to craft a life sharing those stories, mine and so many others, is a privilege and an honor I give thanks for each and every day.